Big Cats

Grayscale Adult Coloring Book

by
Patricia Markham

Thank you for purchasing "Big Cats." If you enjoy this book of designs, please take a moment to give it a 5 star rating on Amazon and leave a positive comment. While you're there (on Amazon) look for other books by Patricia Markham.

Look for other books
by author and illustrator
Patricia Markham

Epiphany Park Publishing
March 2018

Credit for the original designs in this book goes to the many artists who contribute their fine work to the galleries of pixabay.com

Search YouTube for grayscale coloring tutorials or use your browser to search the many websites with tips and instructions on this art form, as well as suggestions for types and brand choices of colored pencils, pens and markers.

Try your colors here.
If you are using pens or markers, it is a good idea to place a blotter or scrap sheet of paper underneath the design you are working on to protect the design behind it. Enjoy!

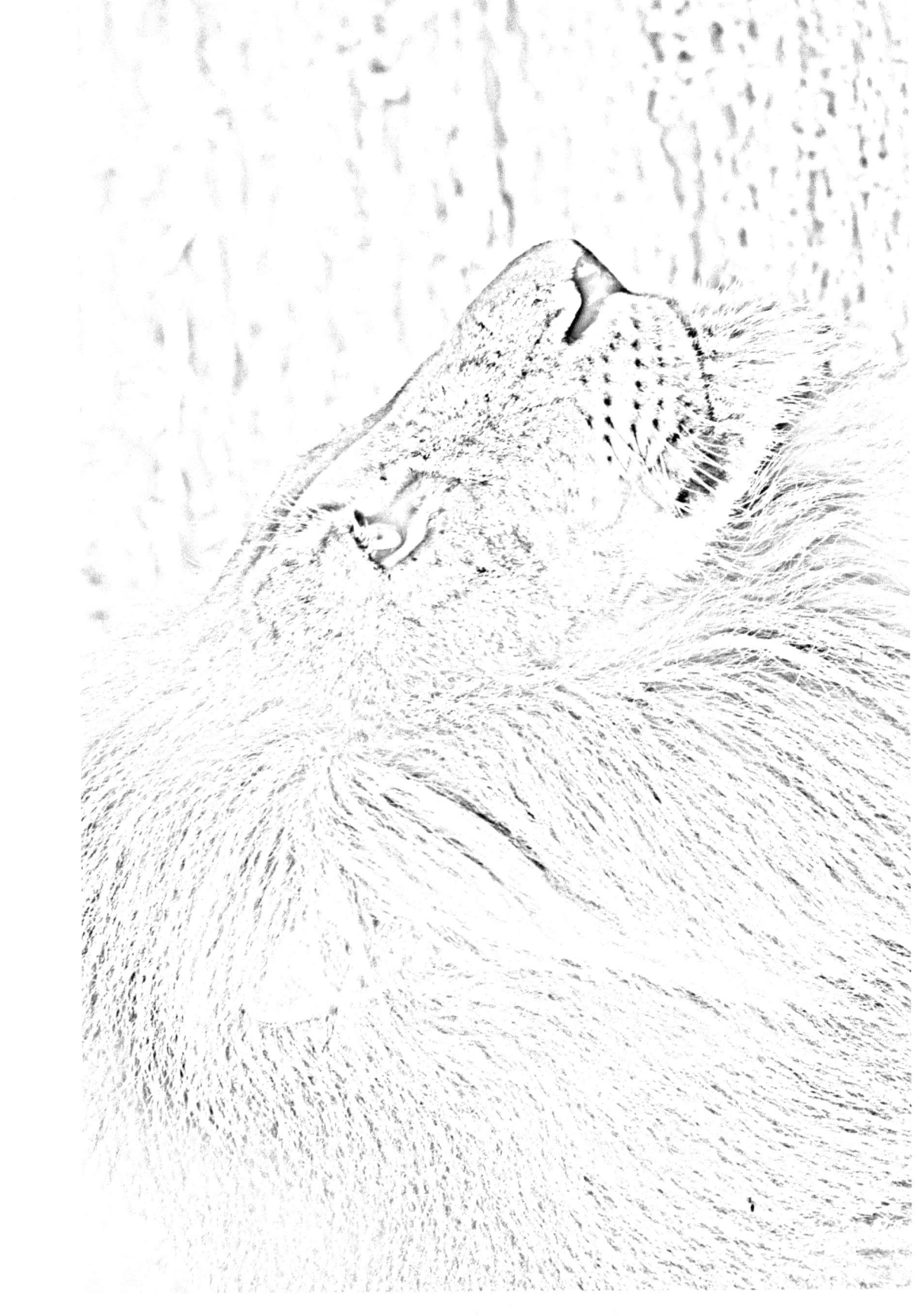

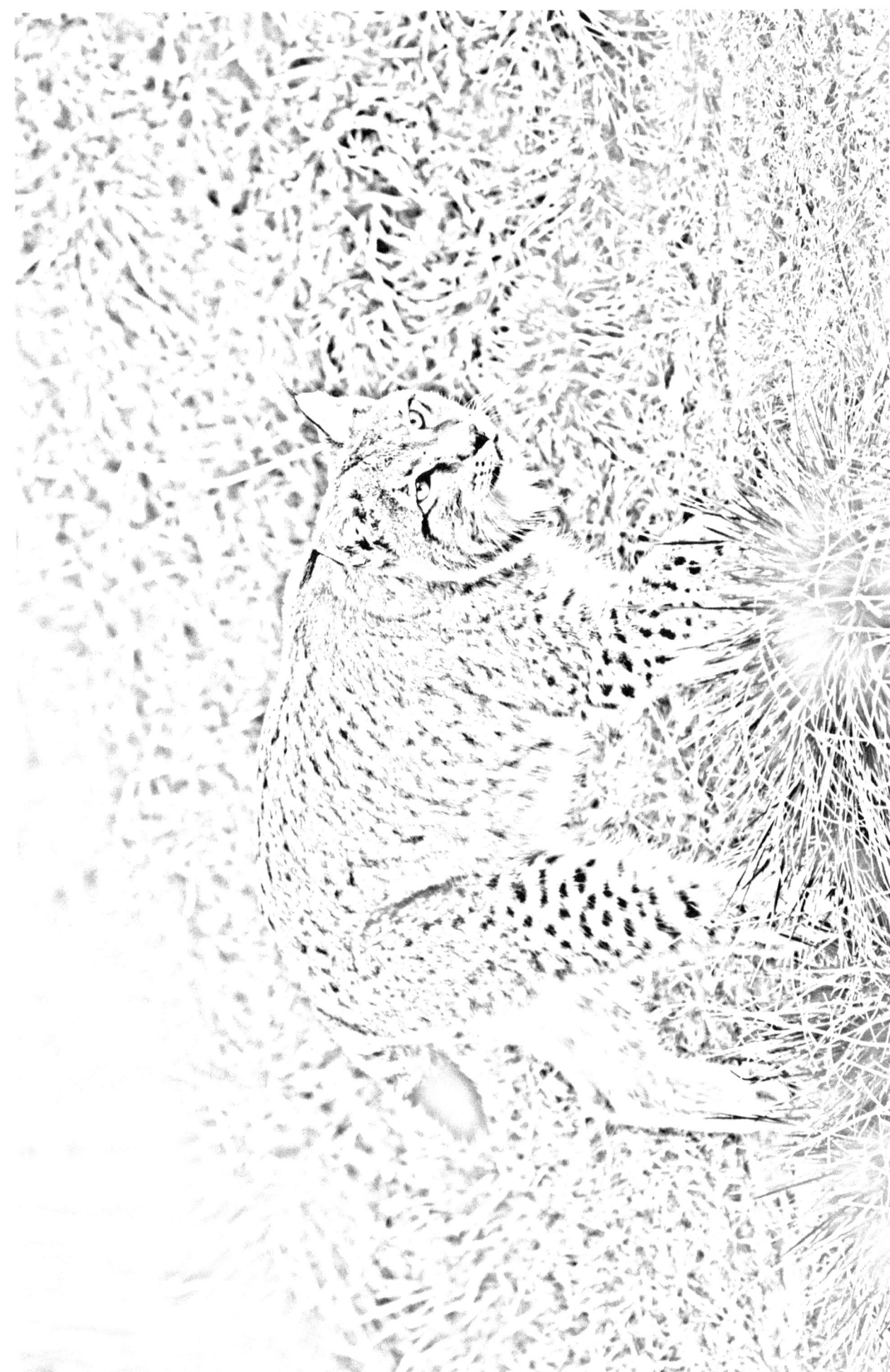

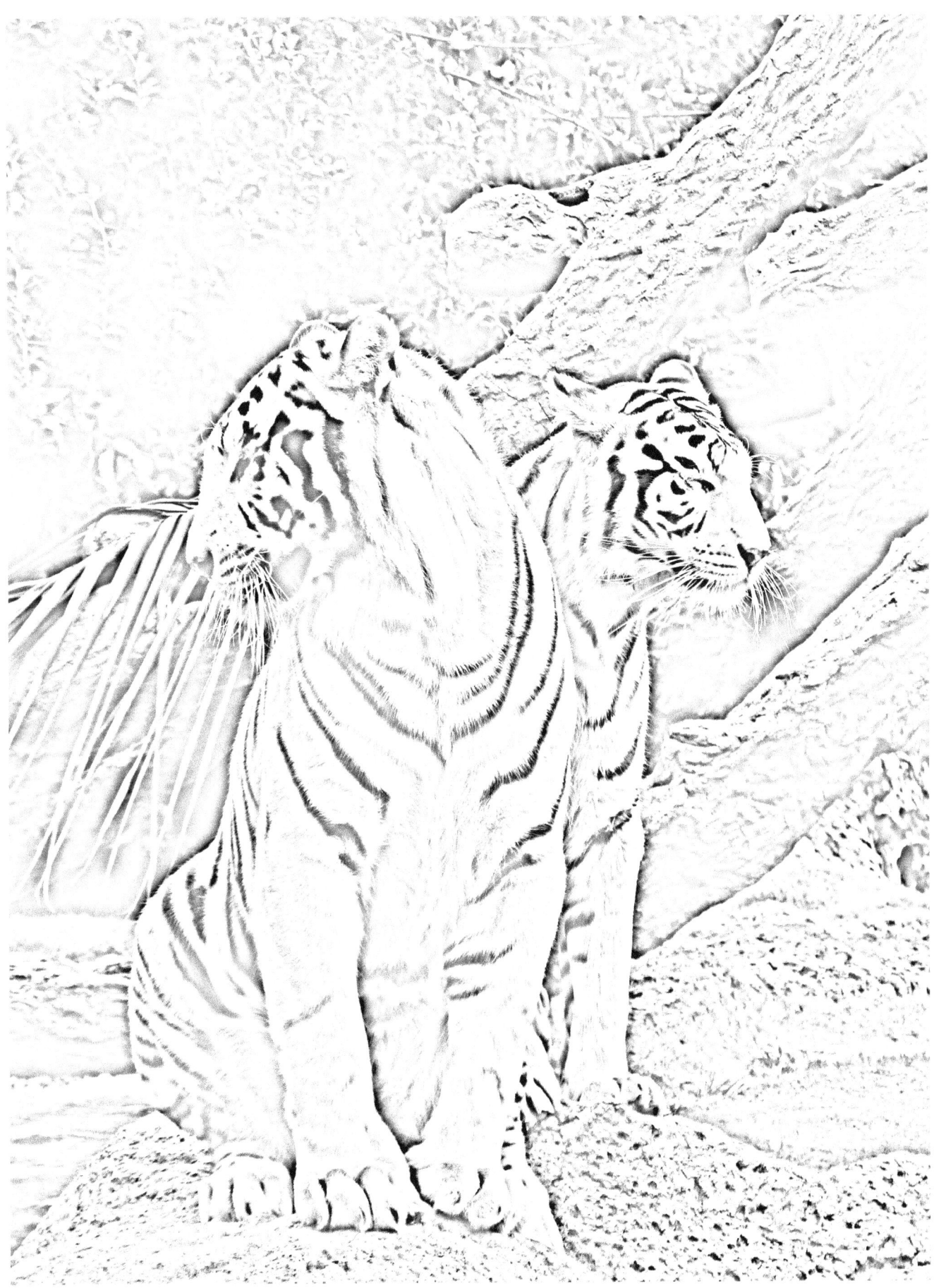

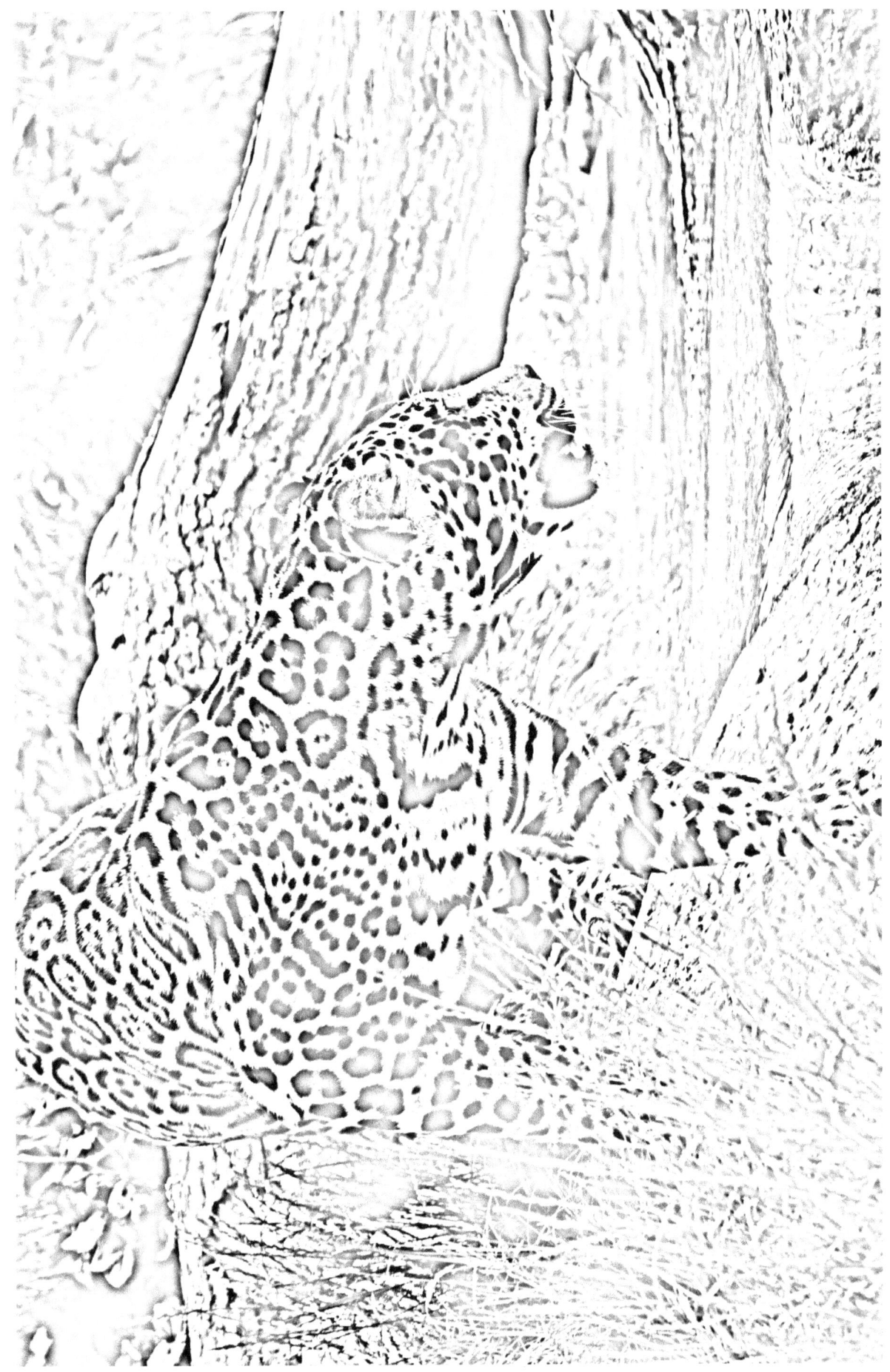

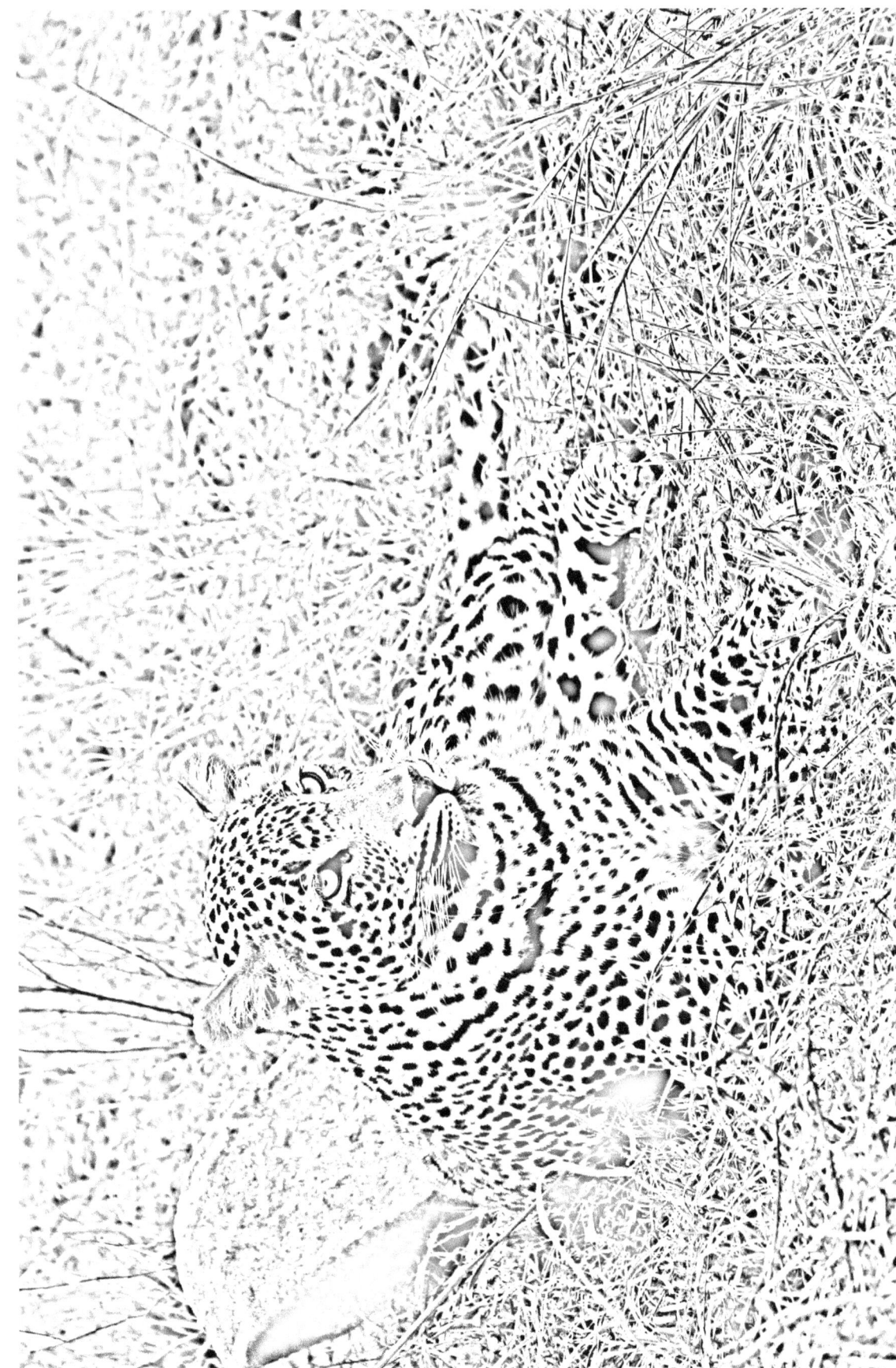

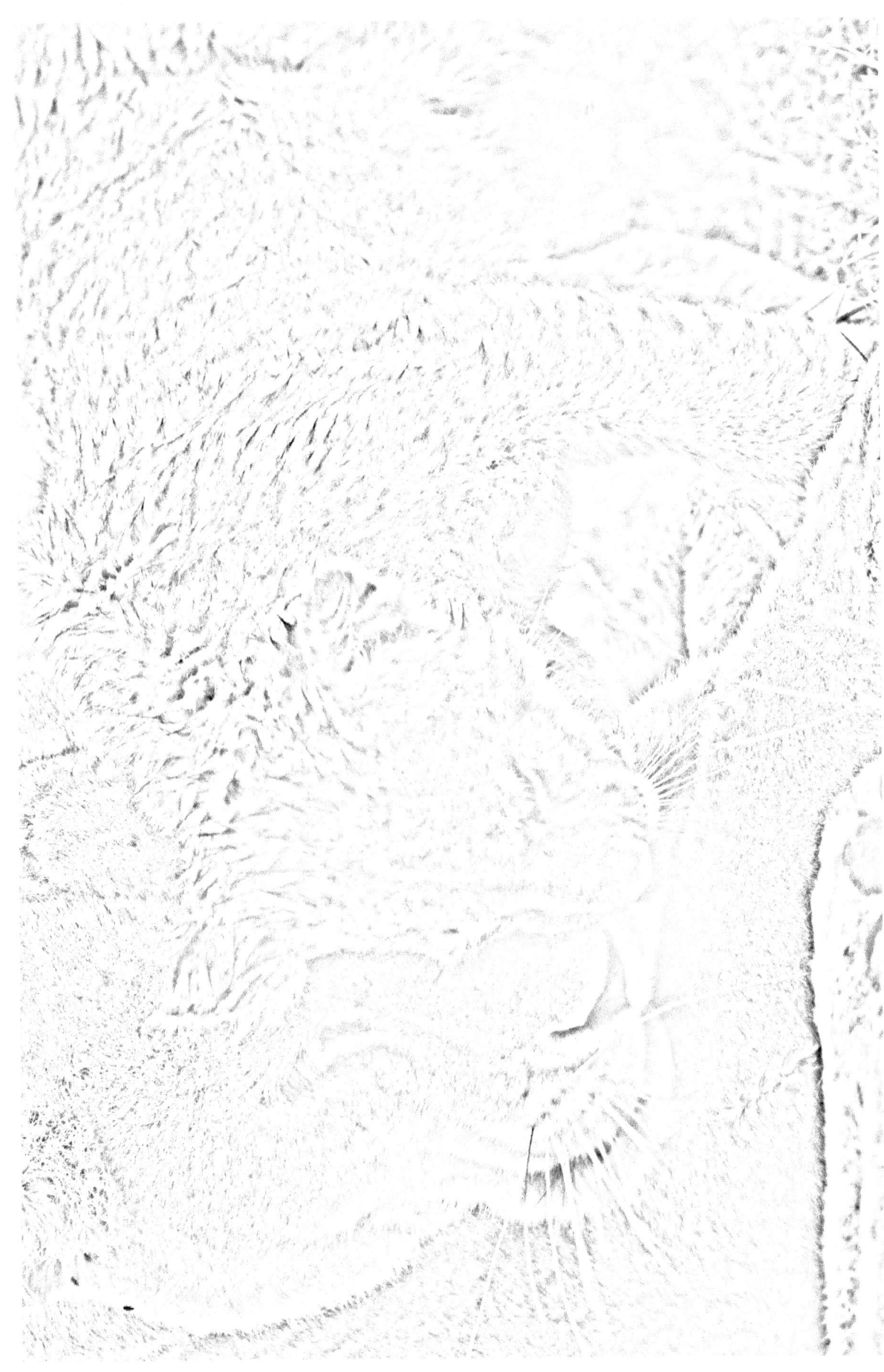

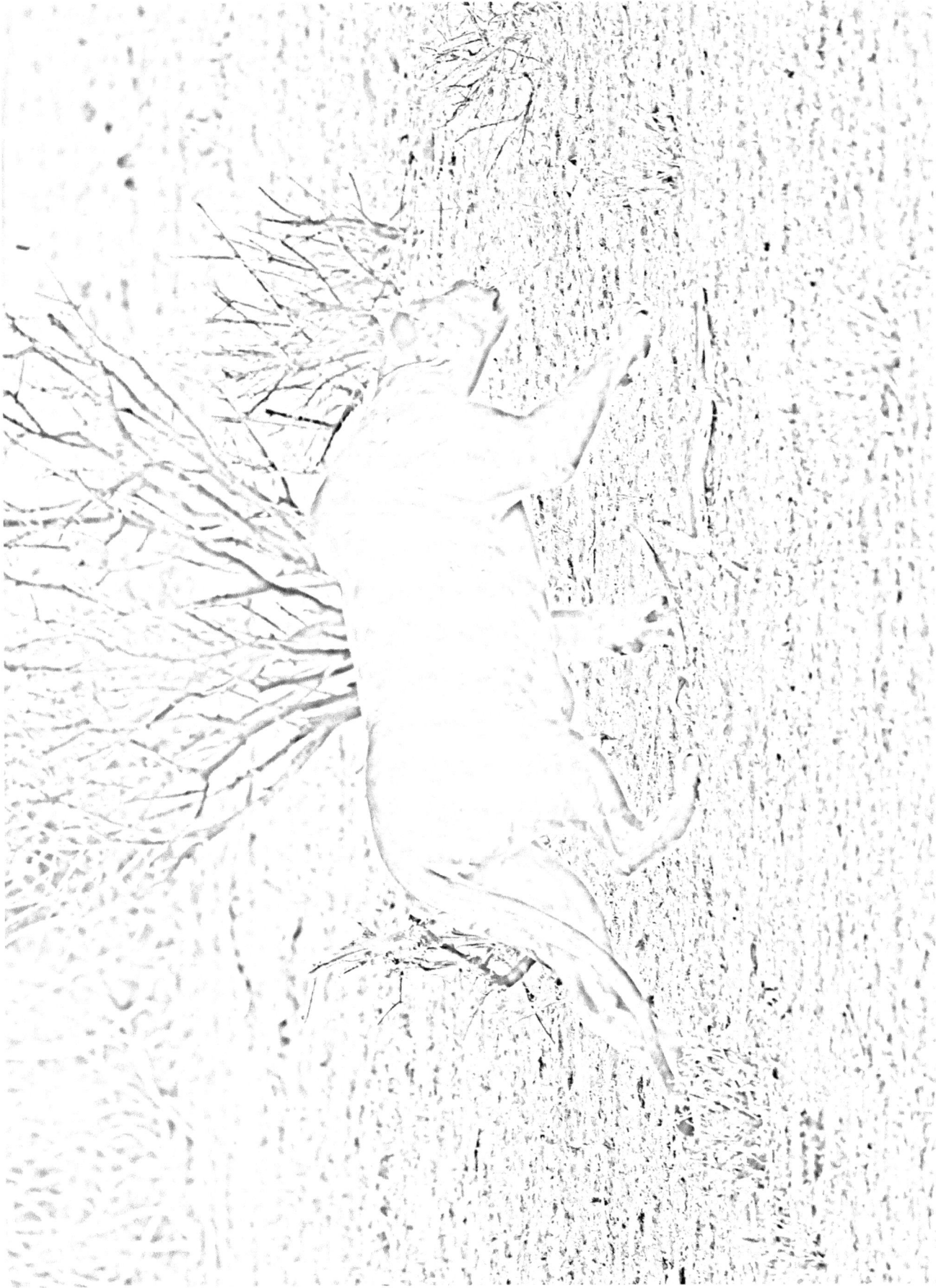

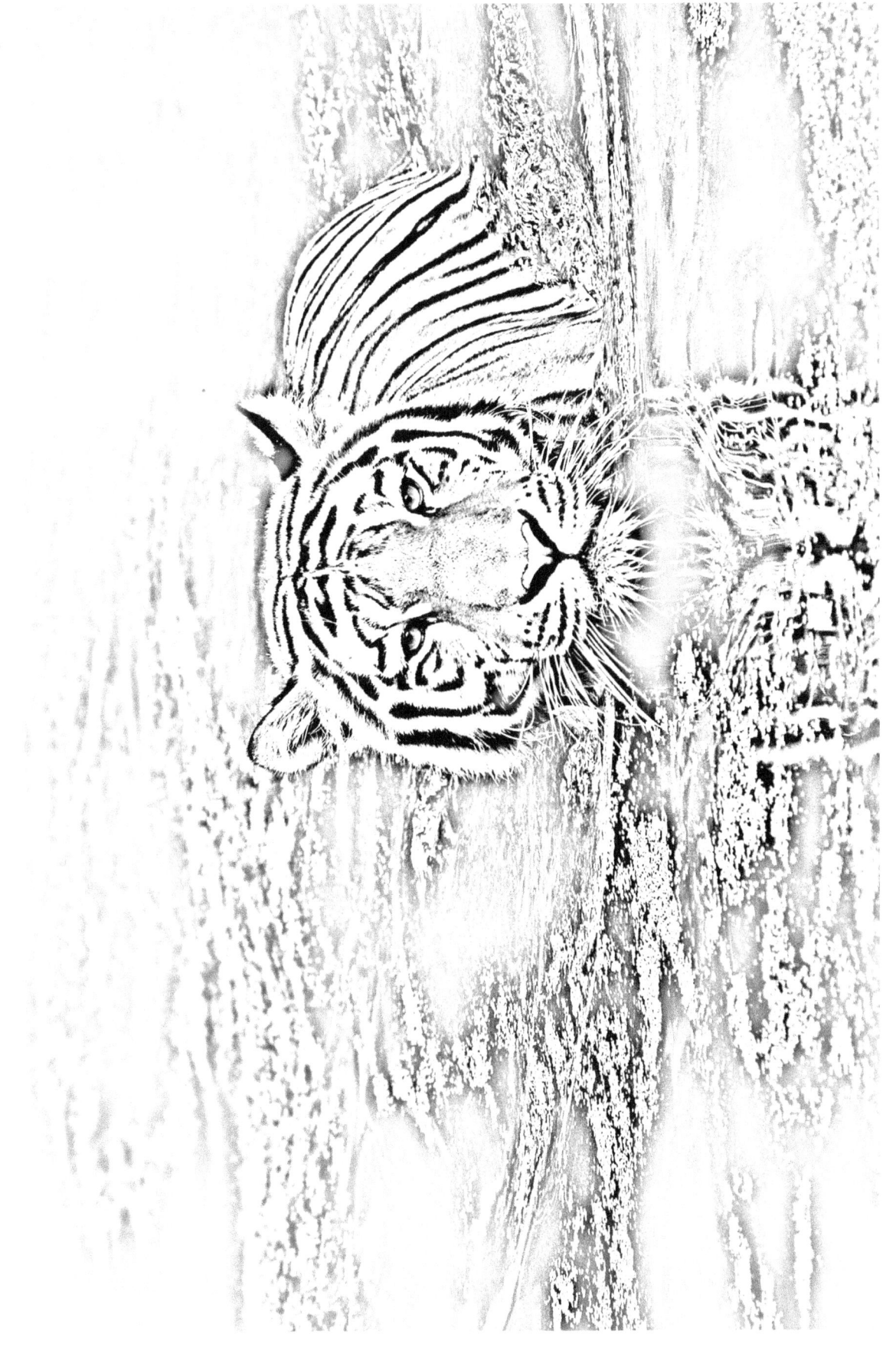

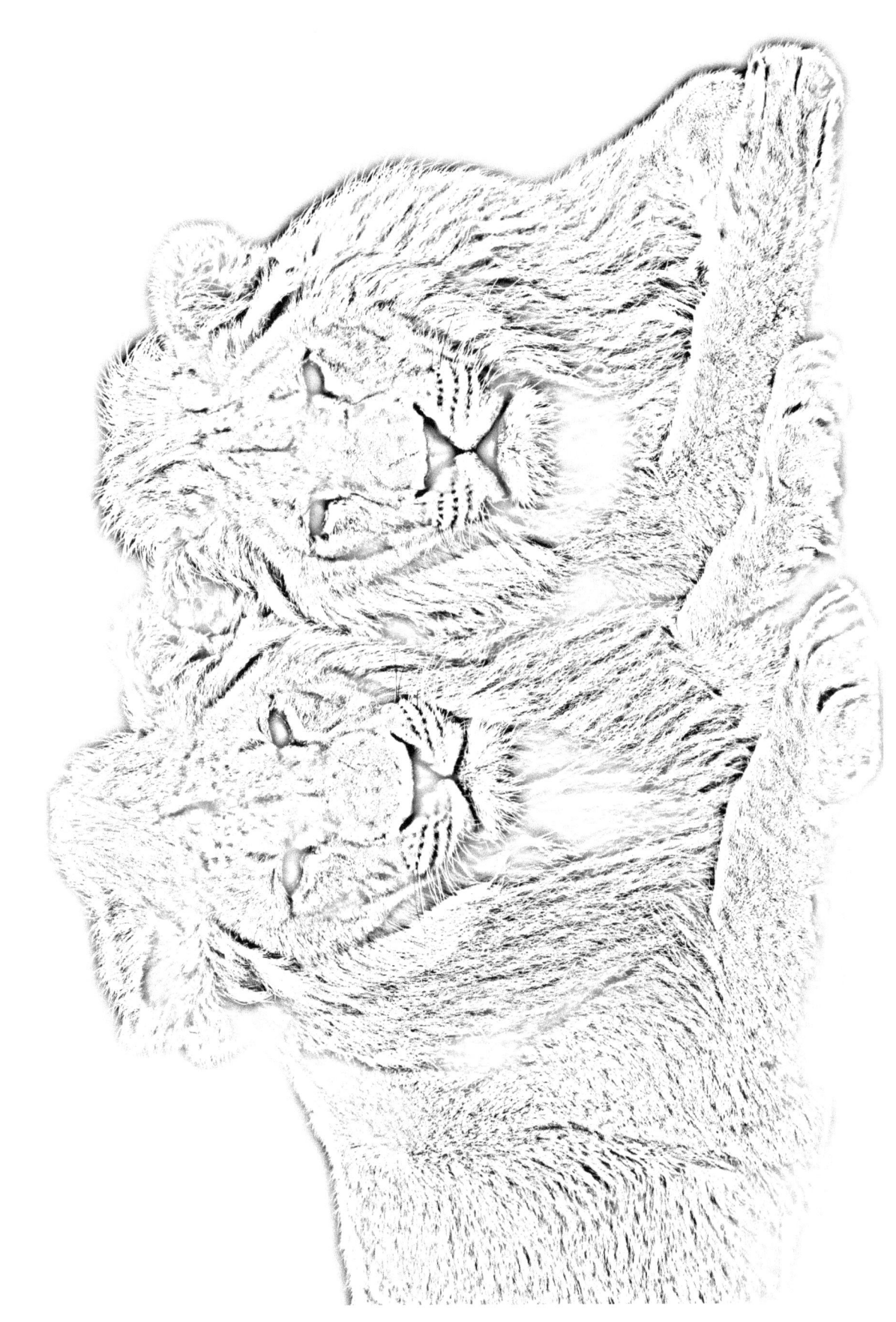

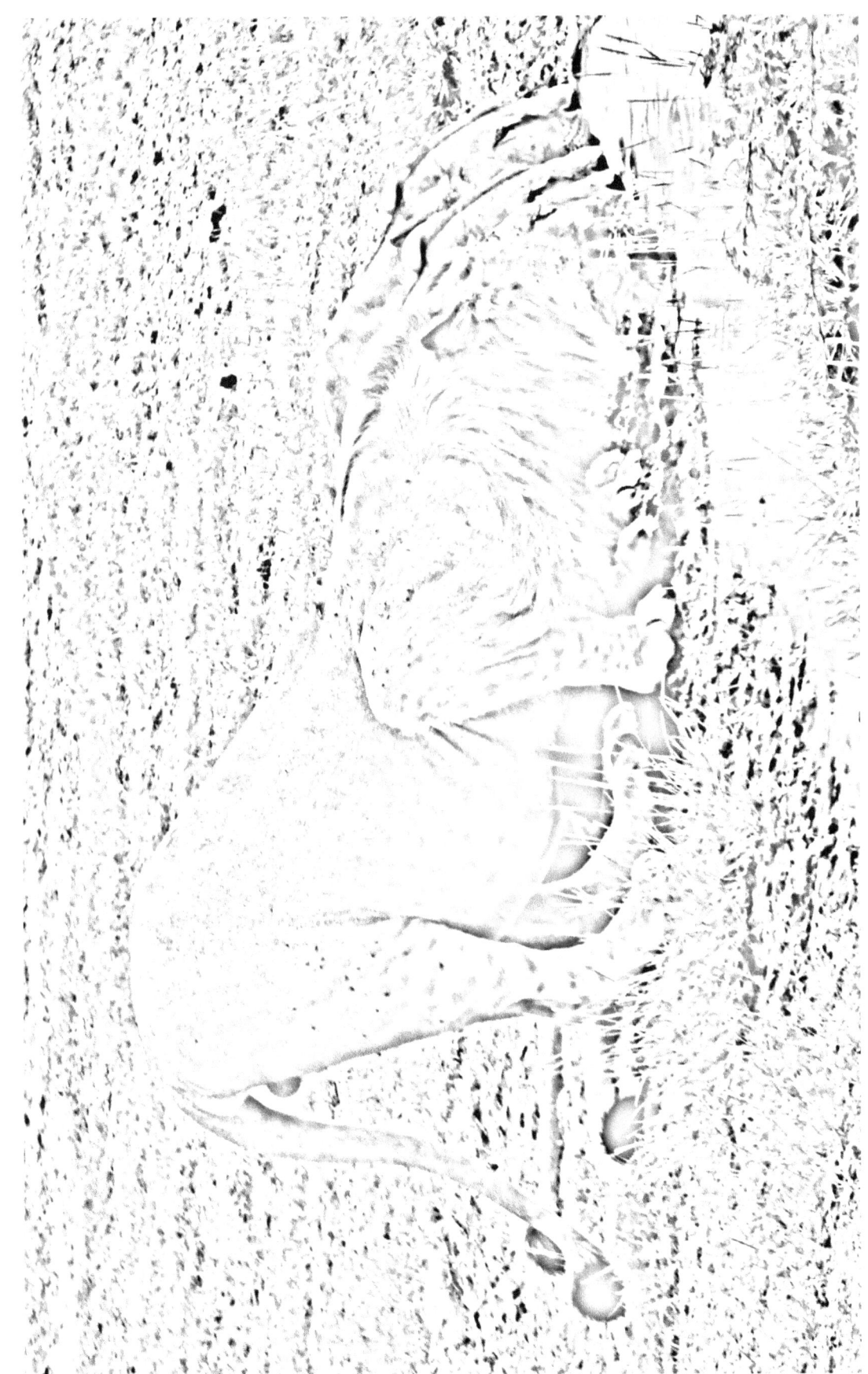

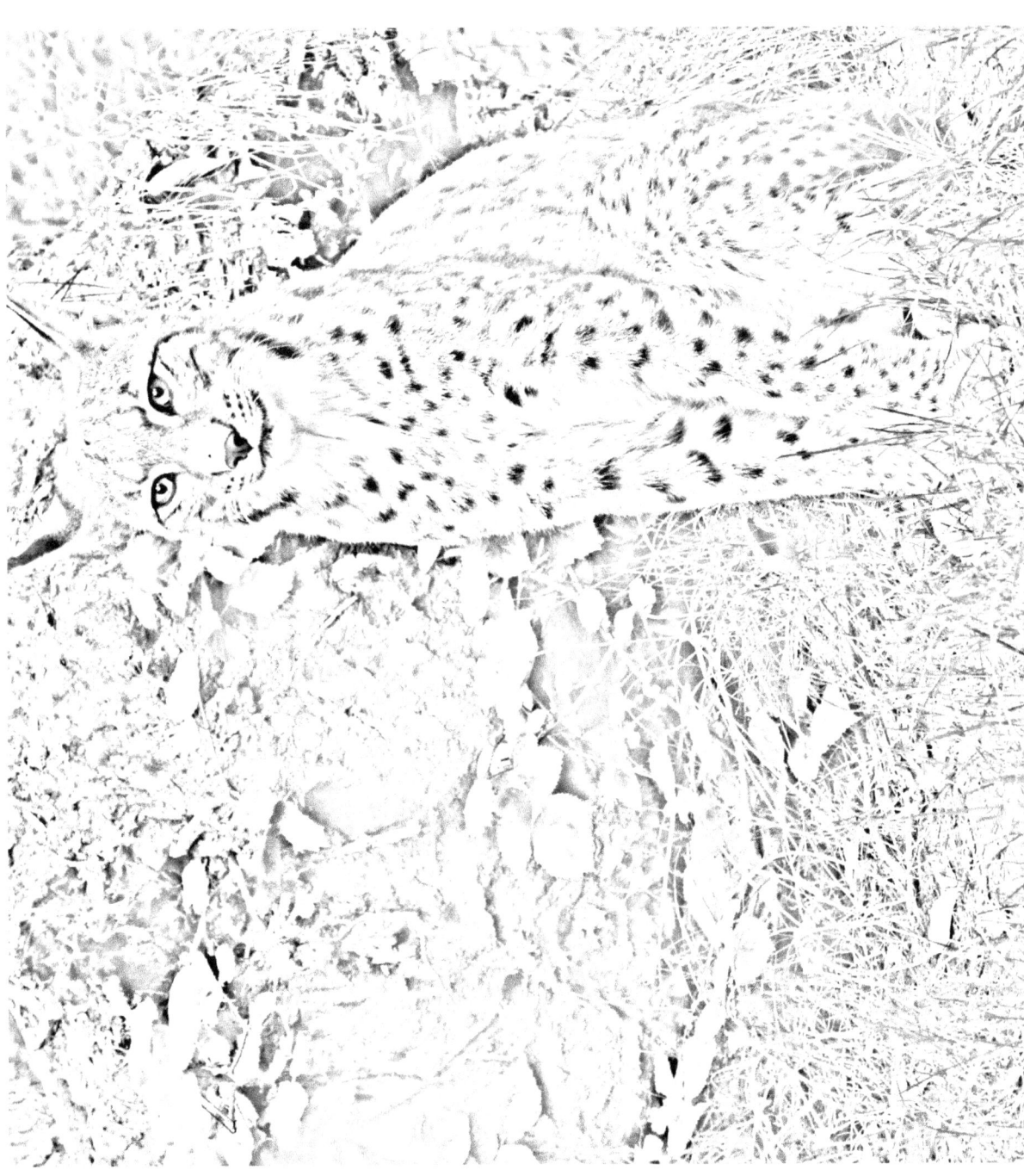

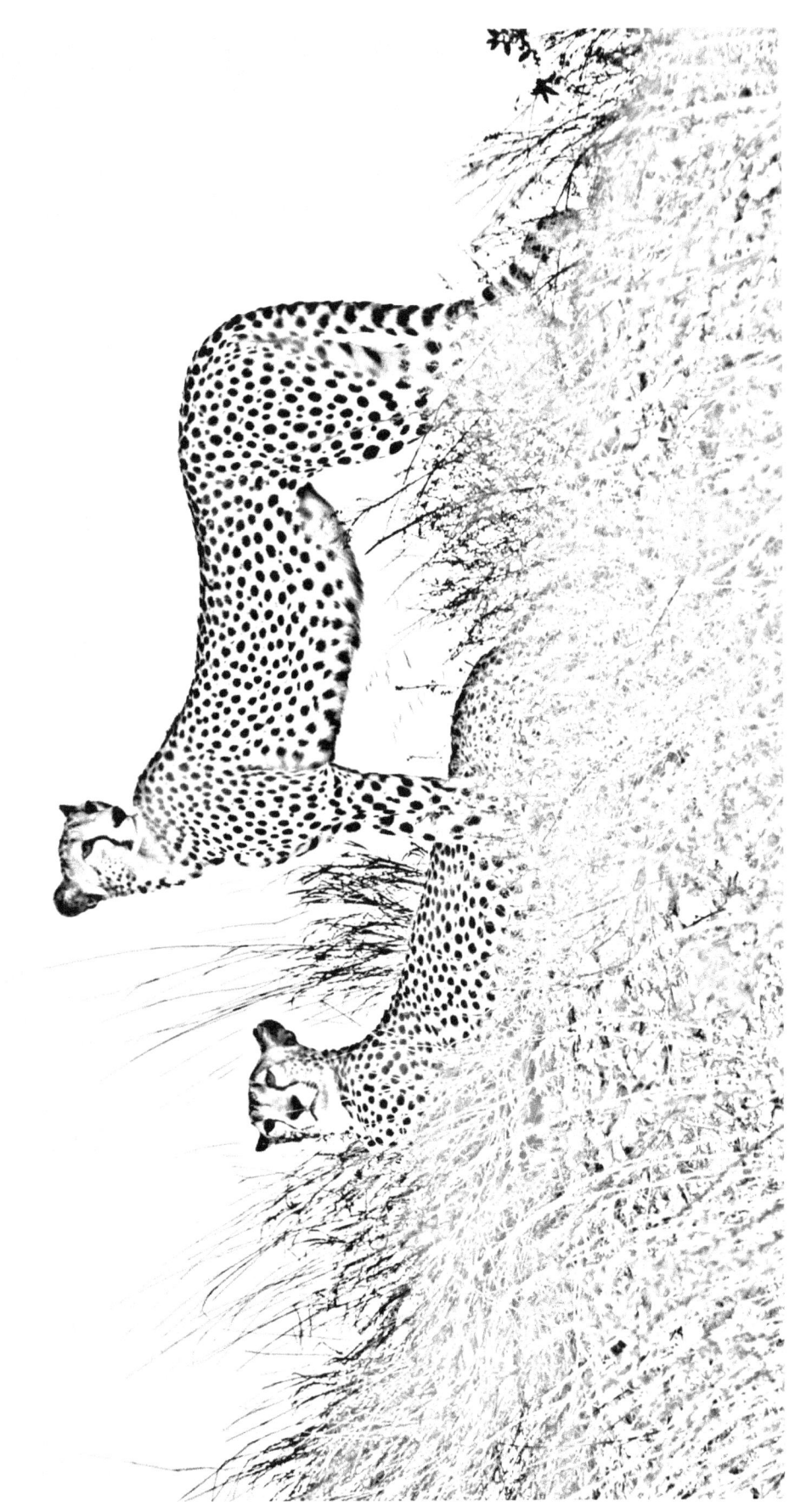

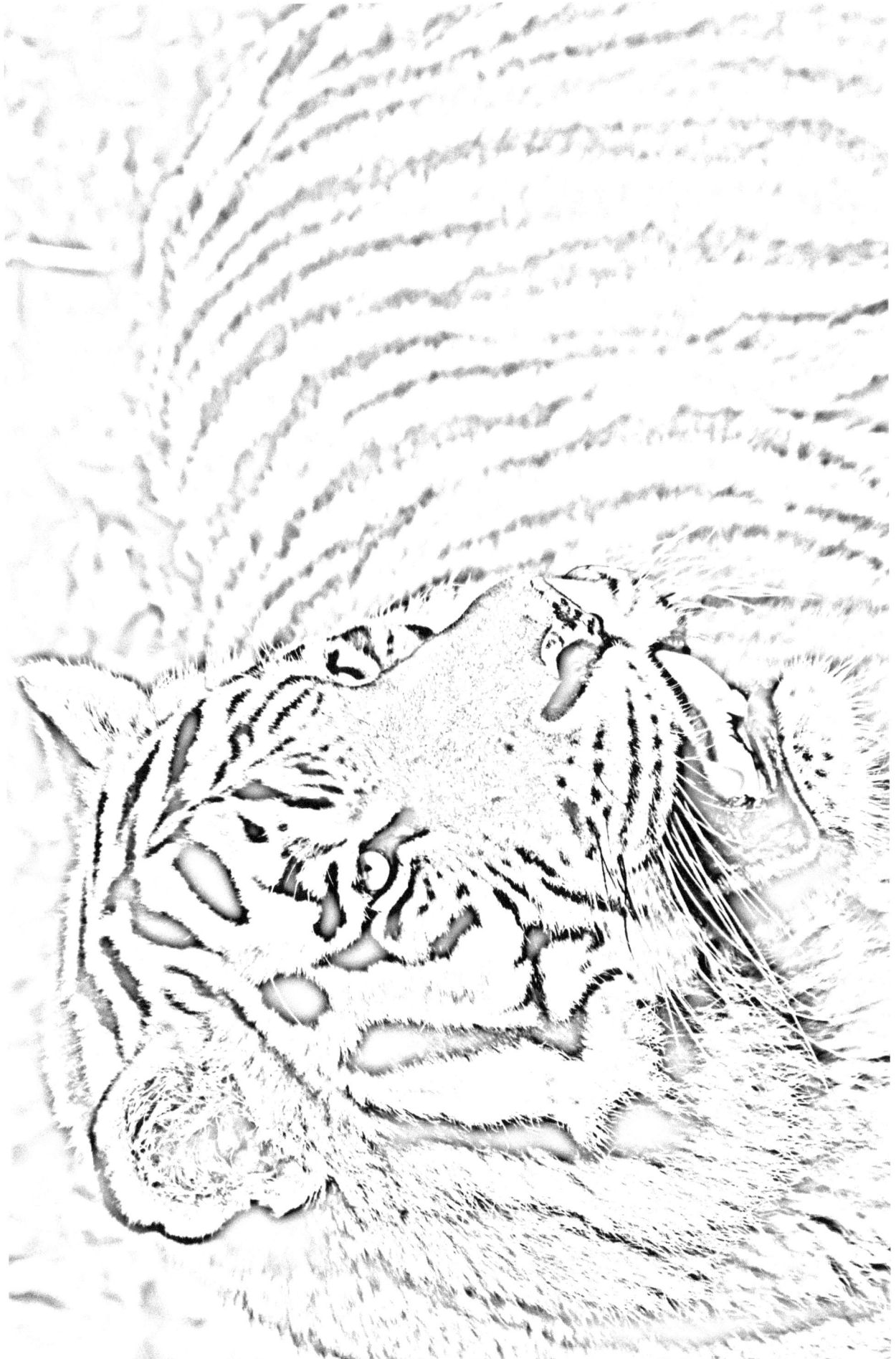

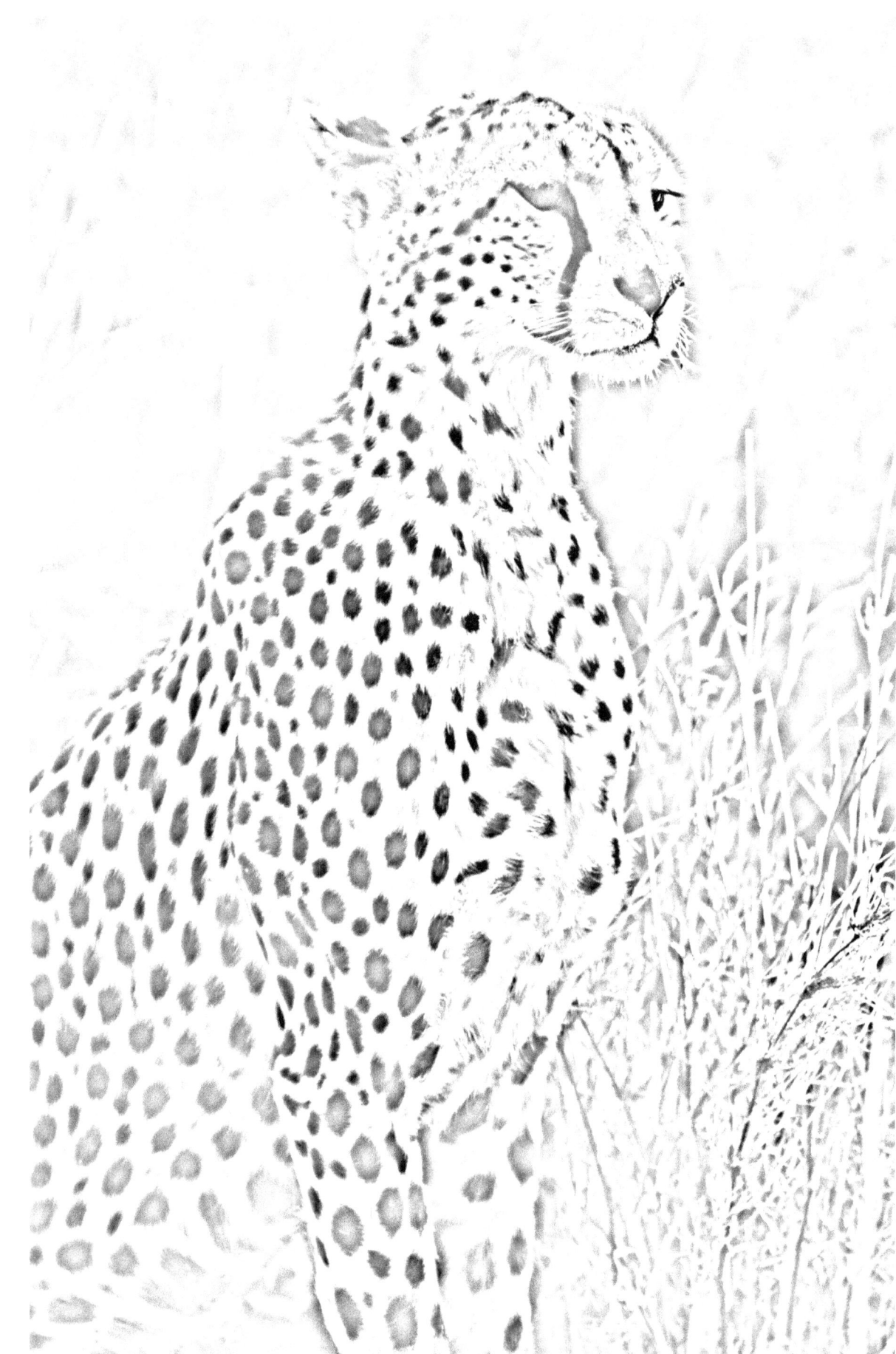

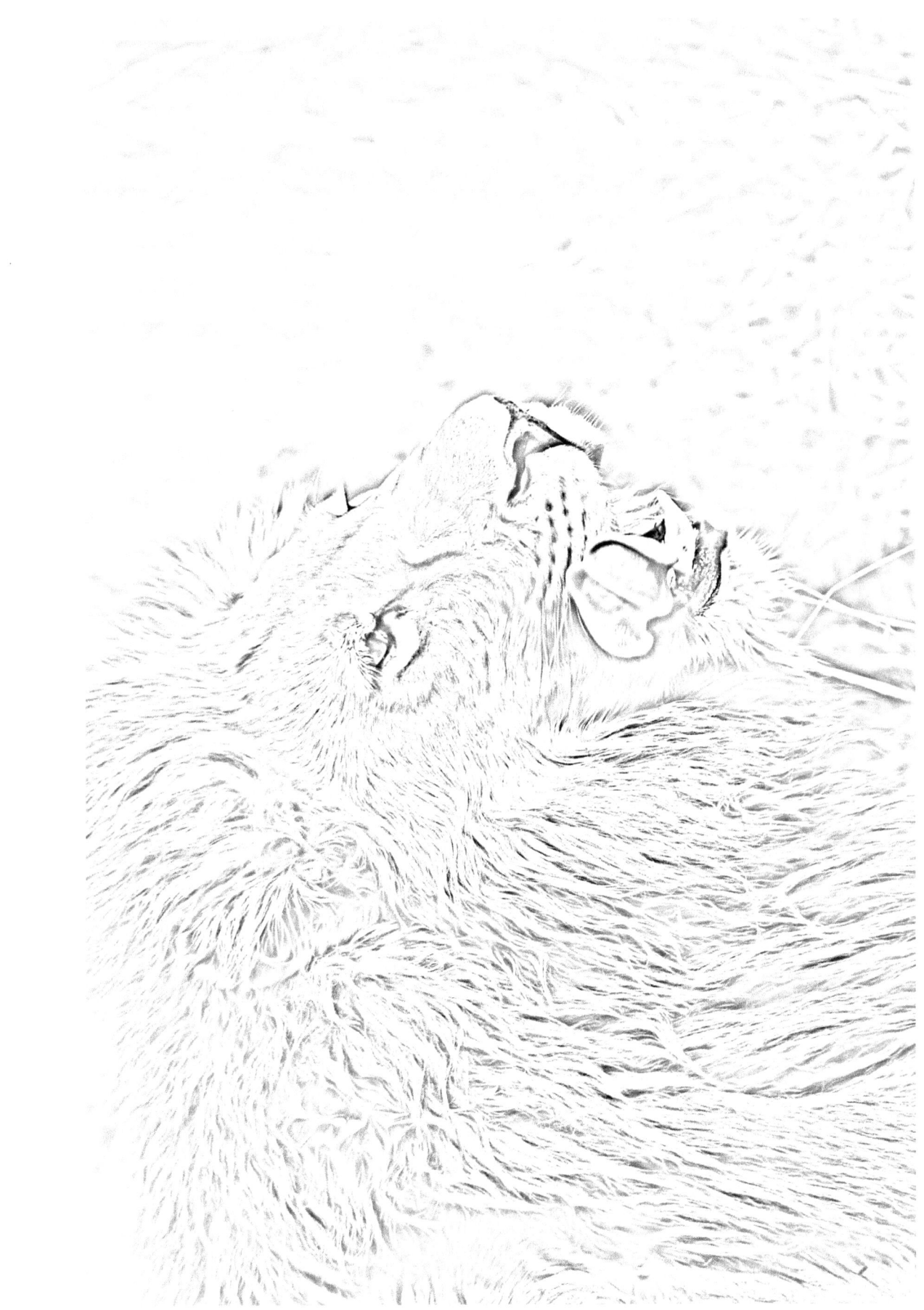

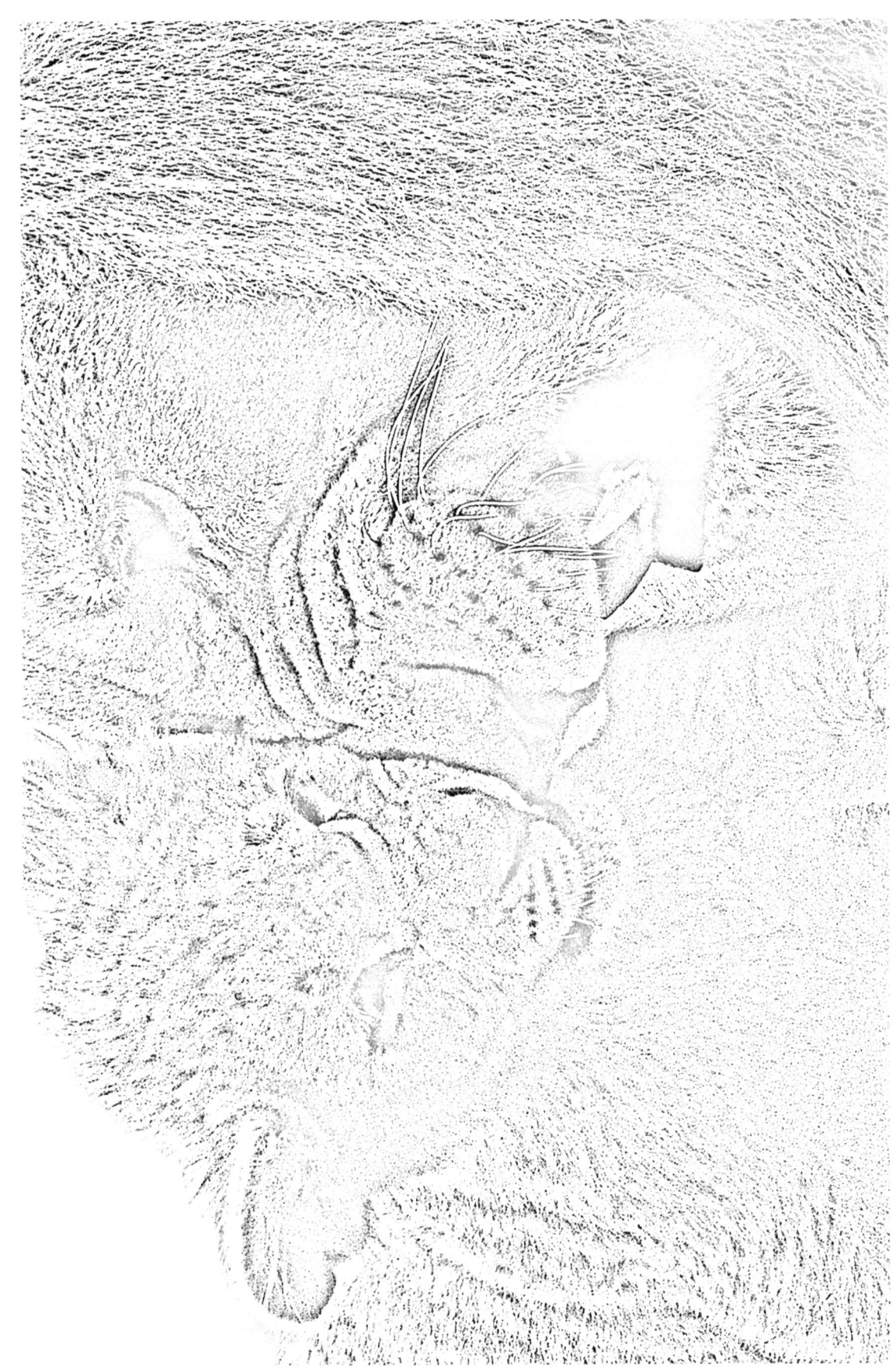

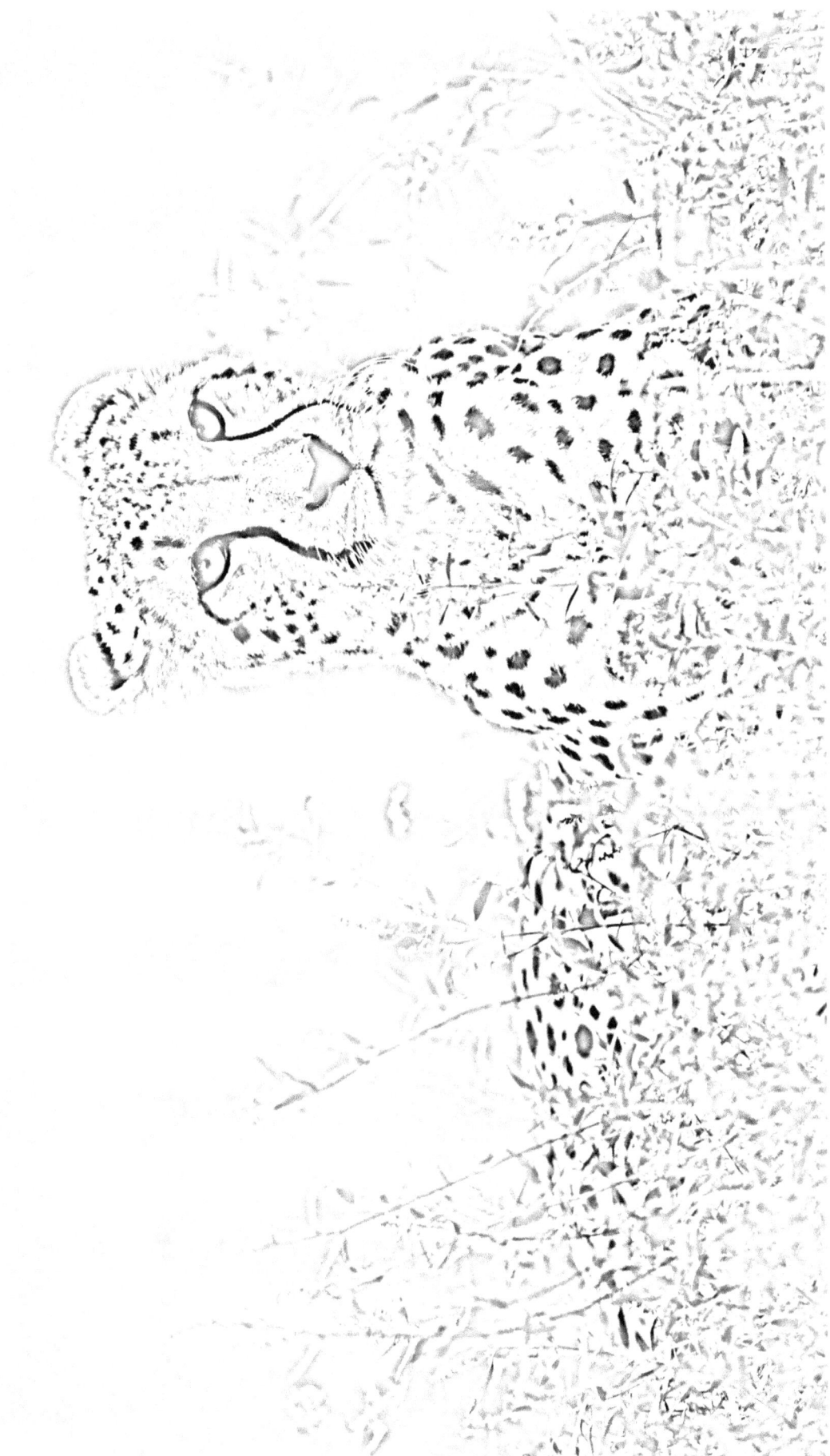

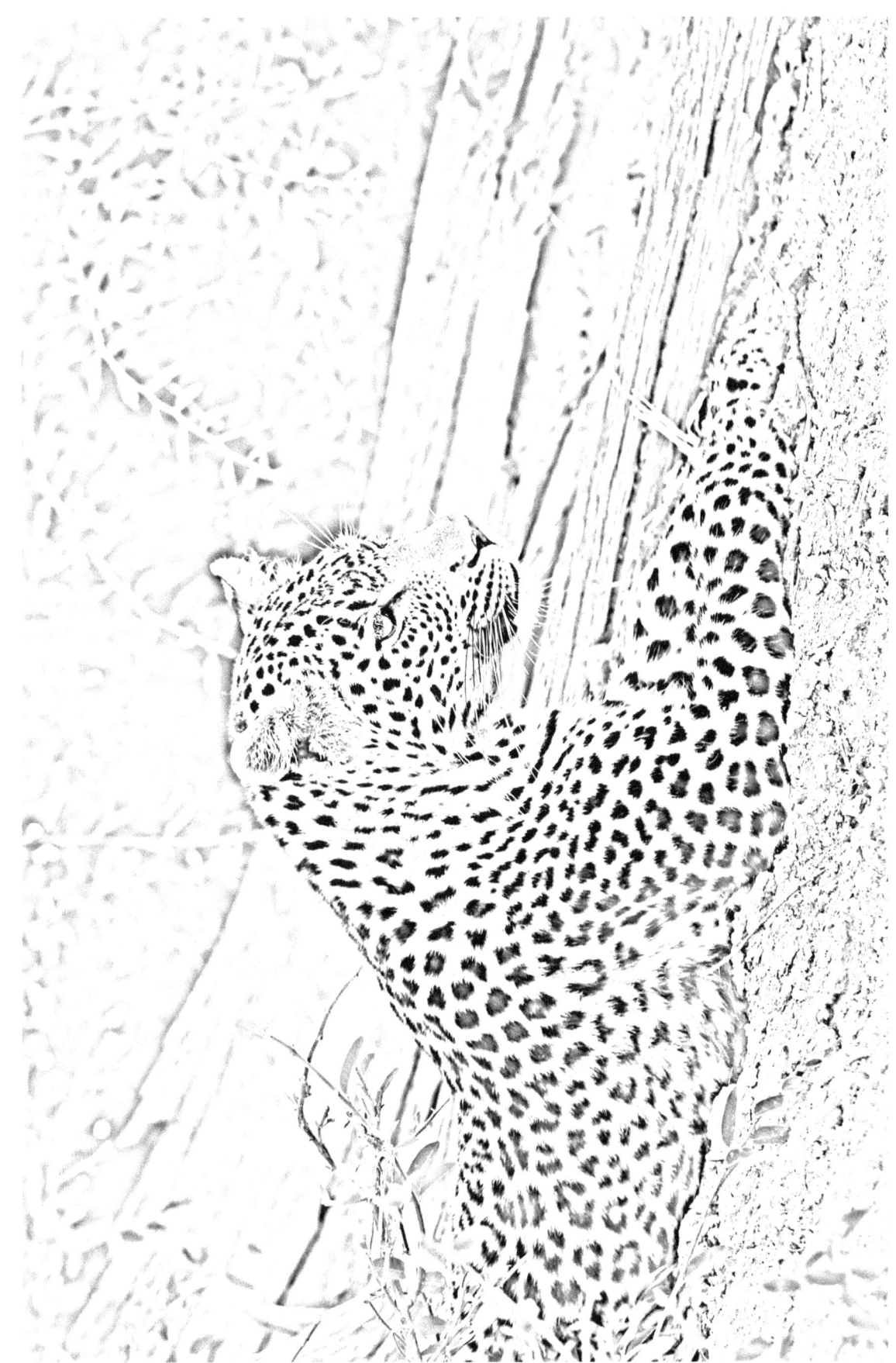

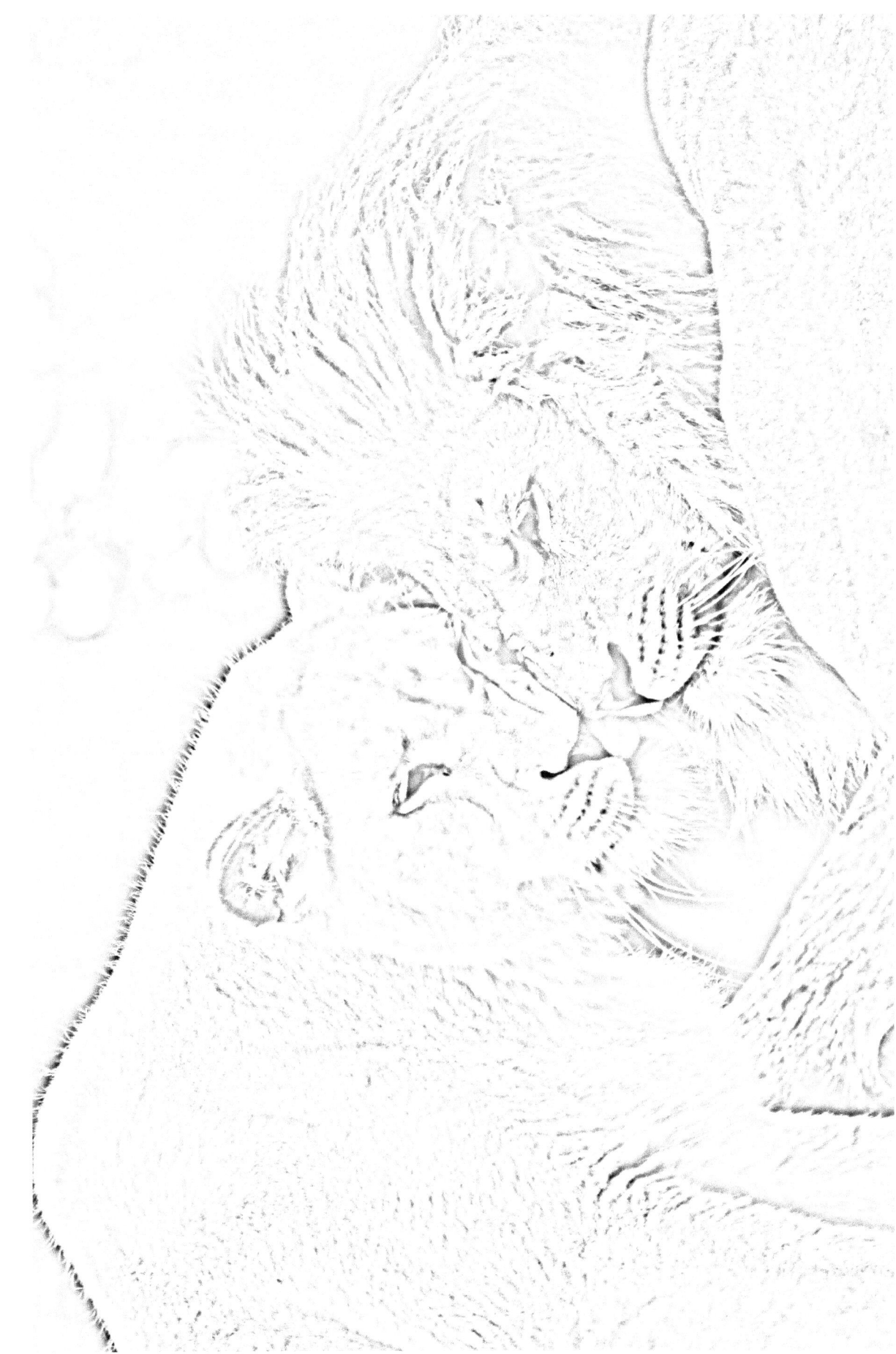

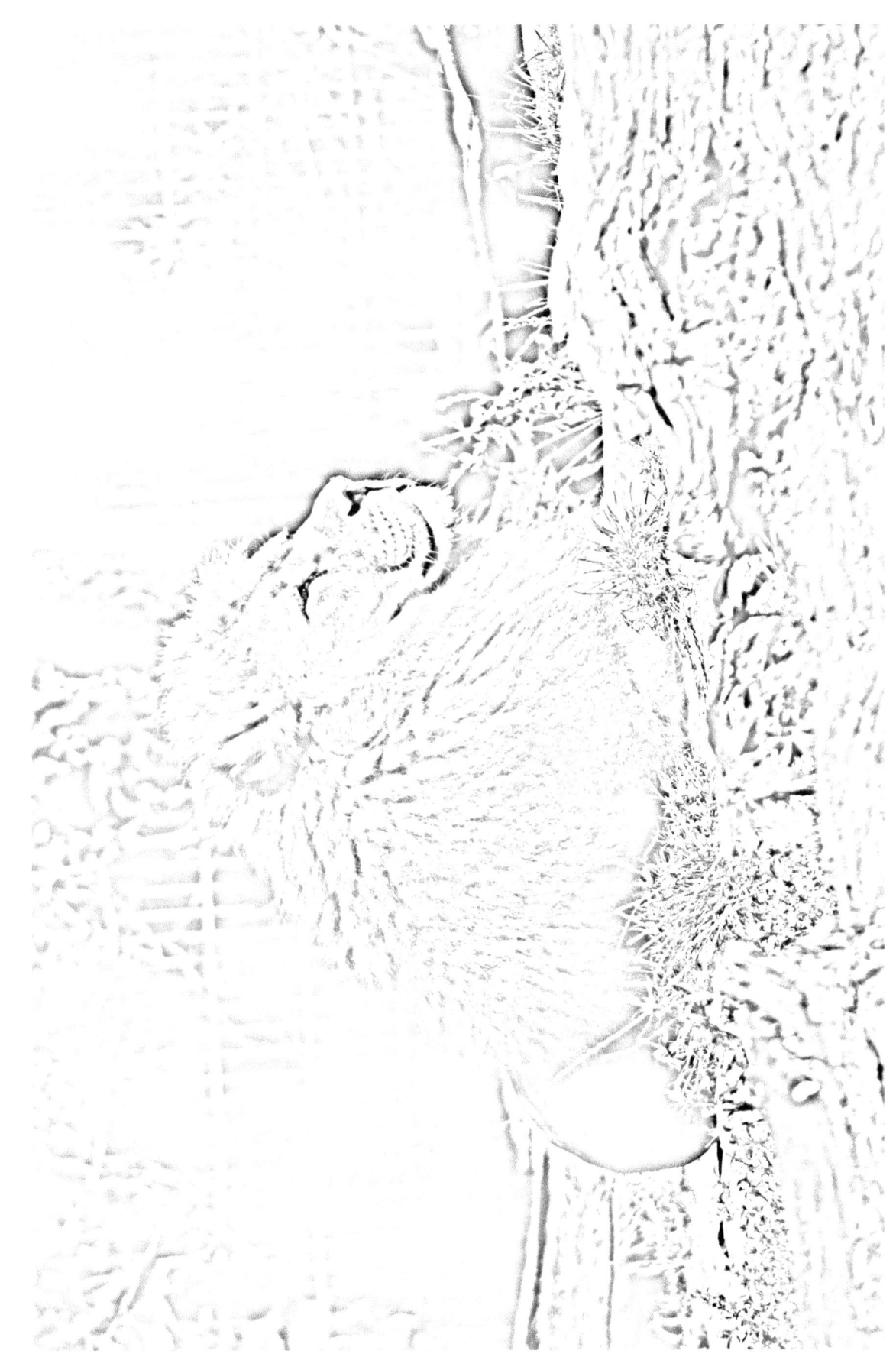

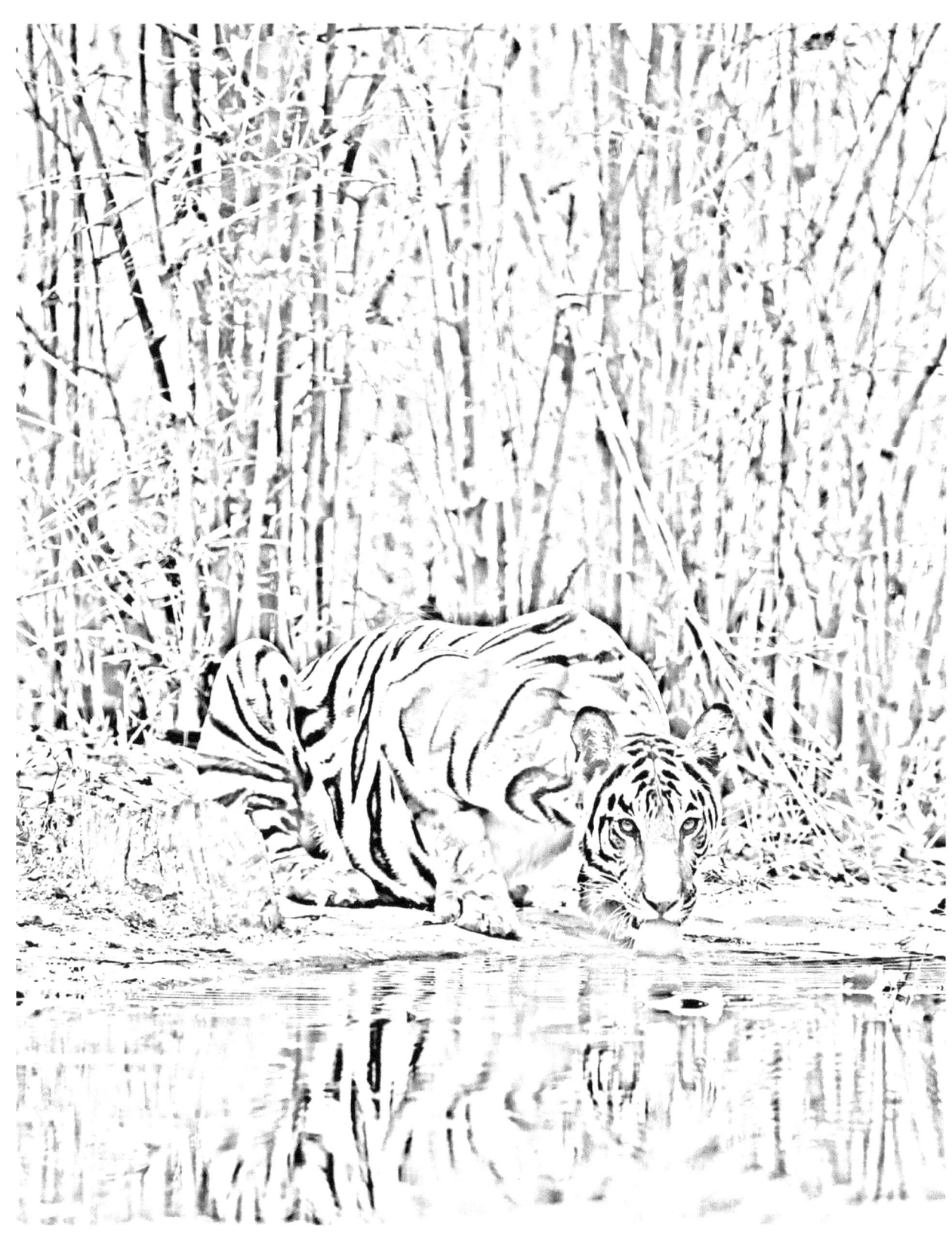

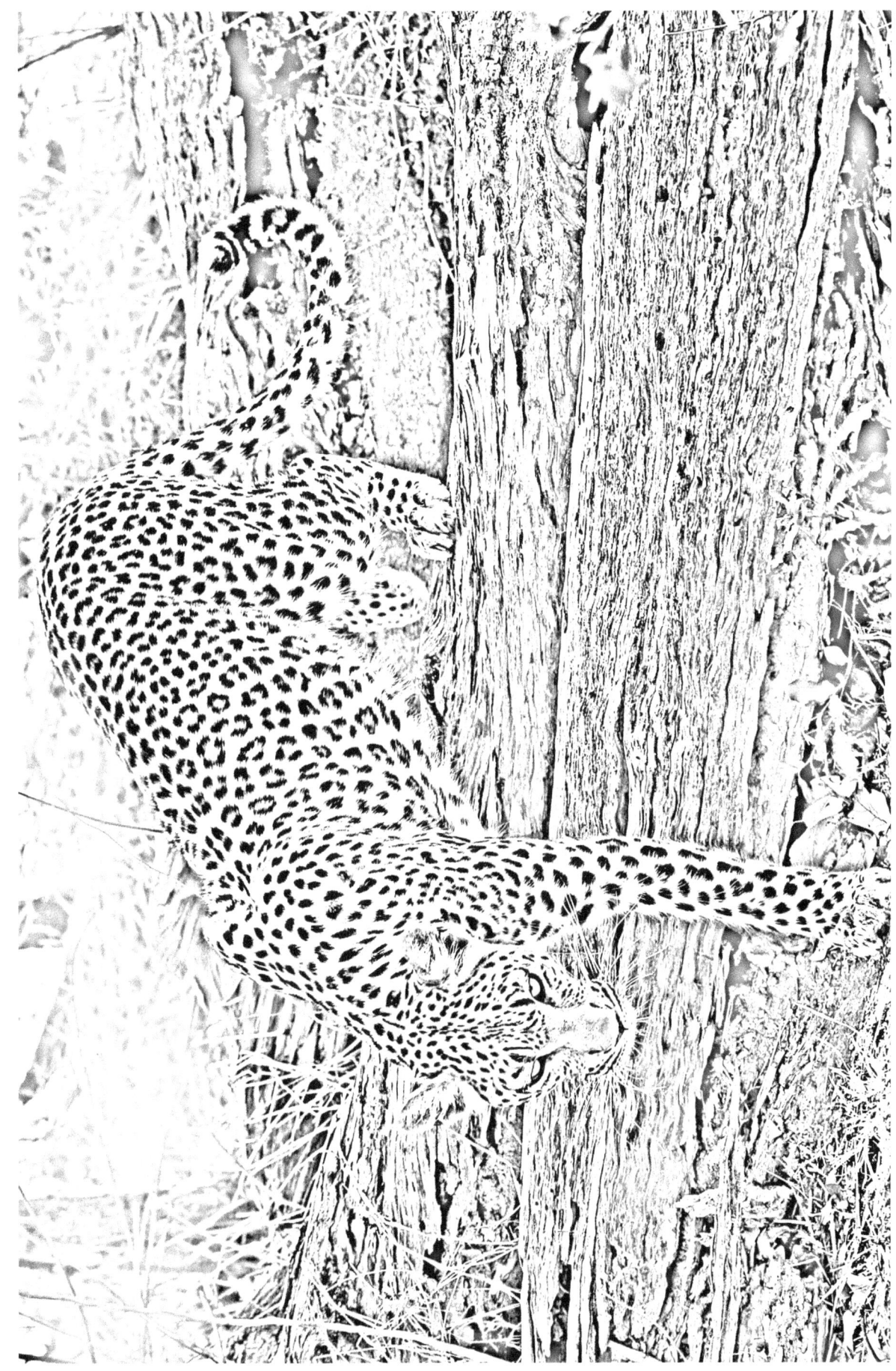

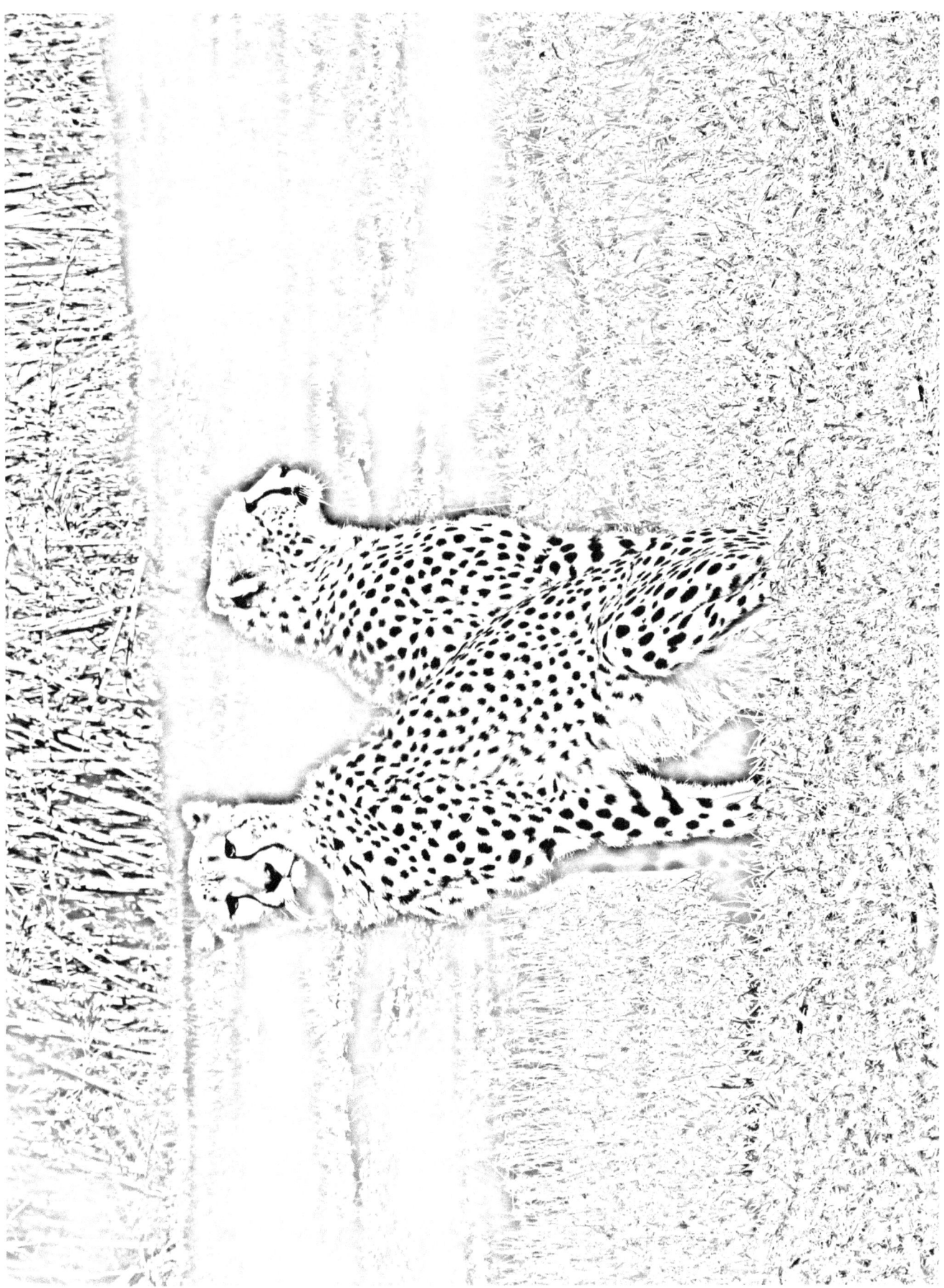

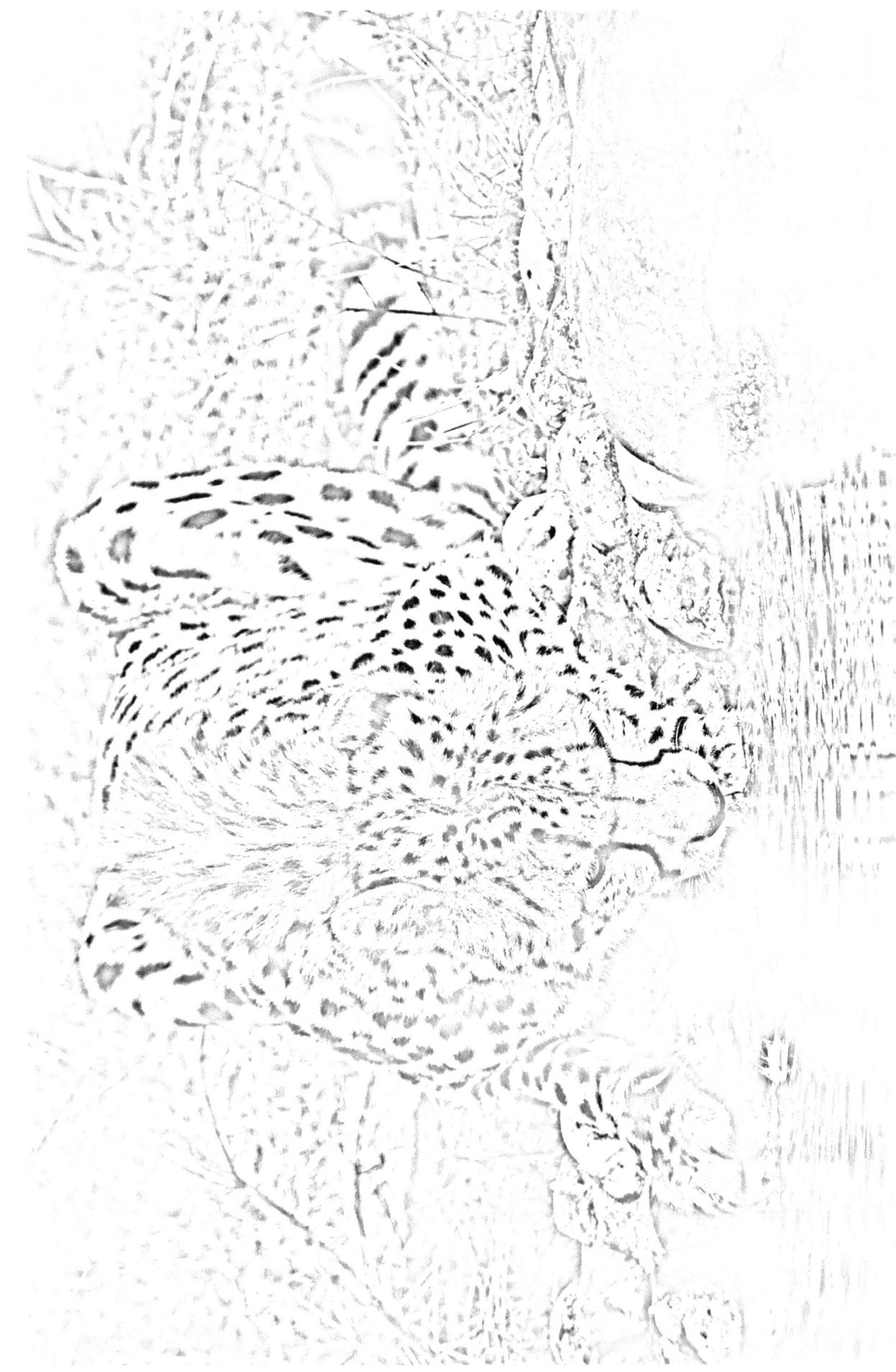

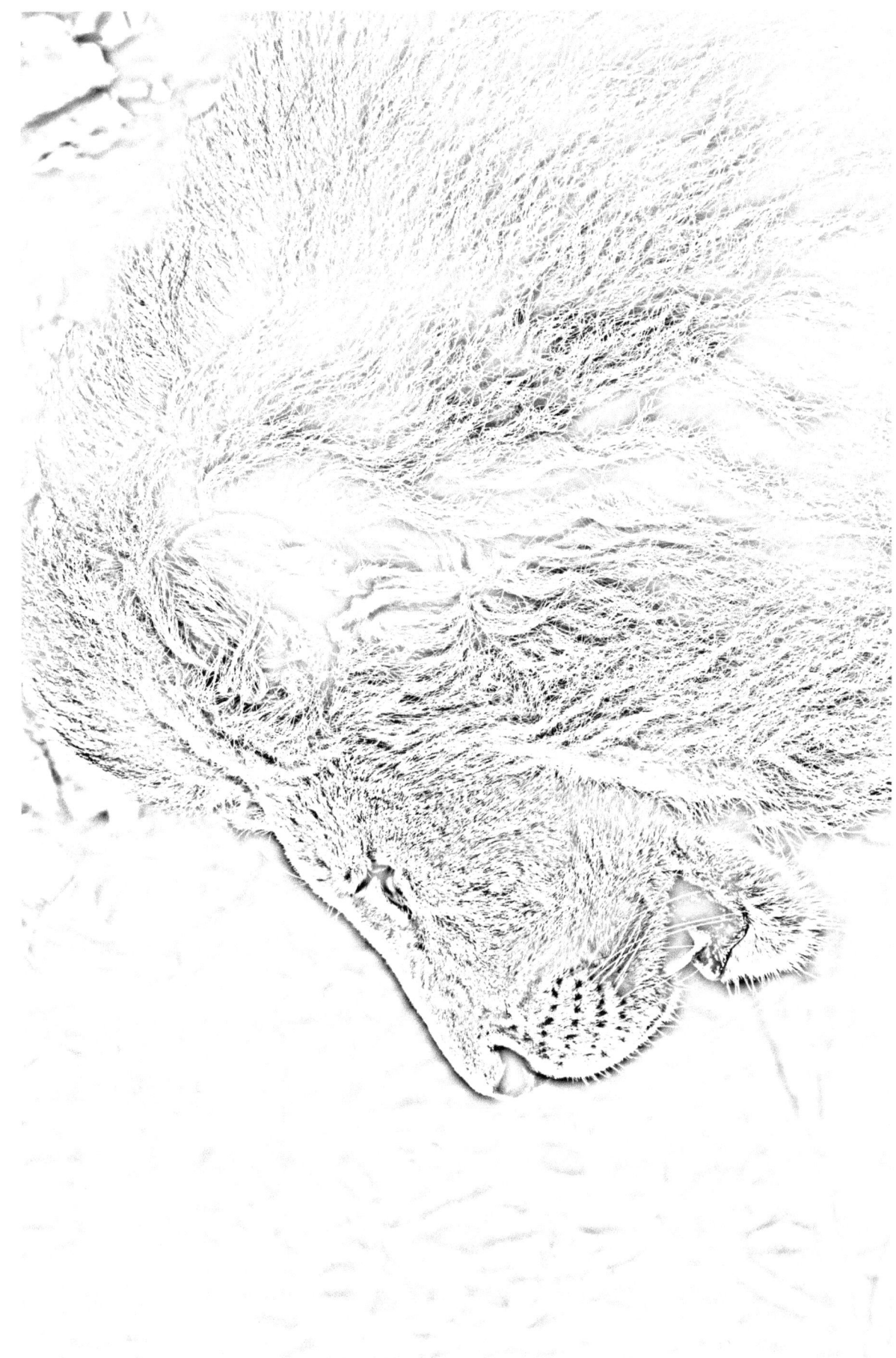

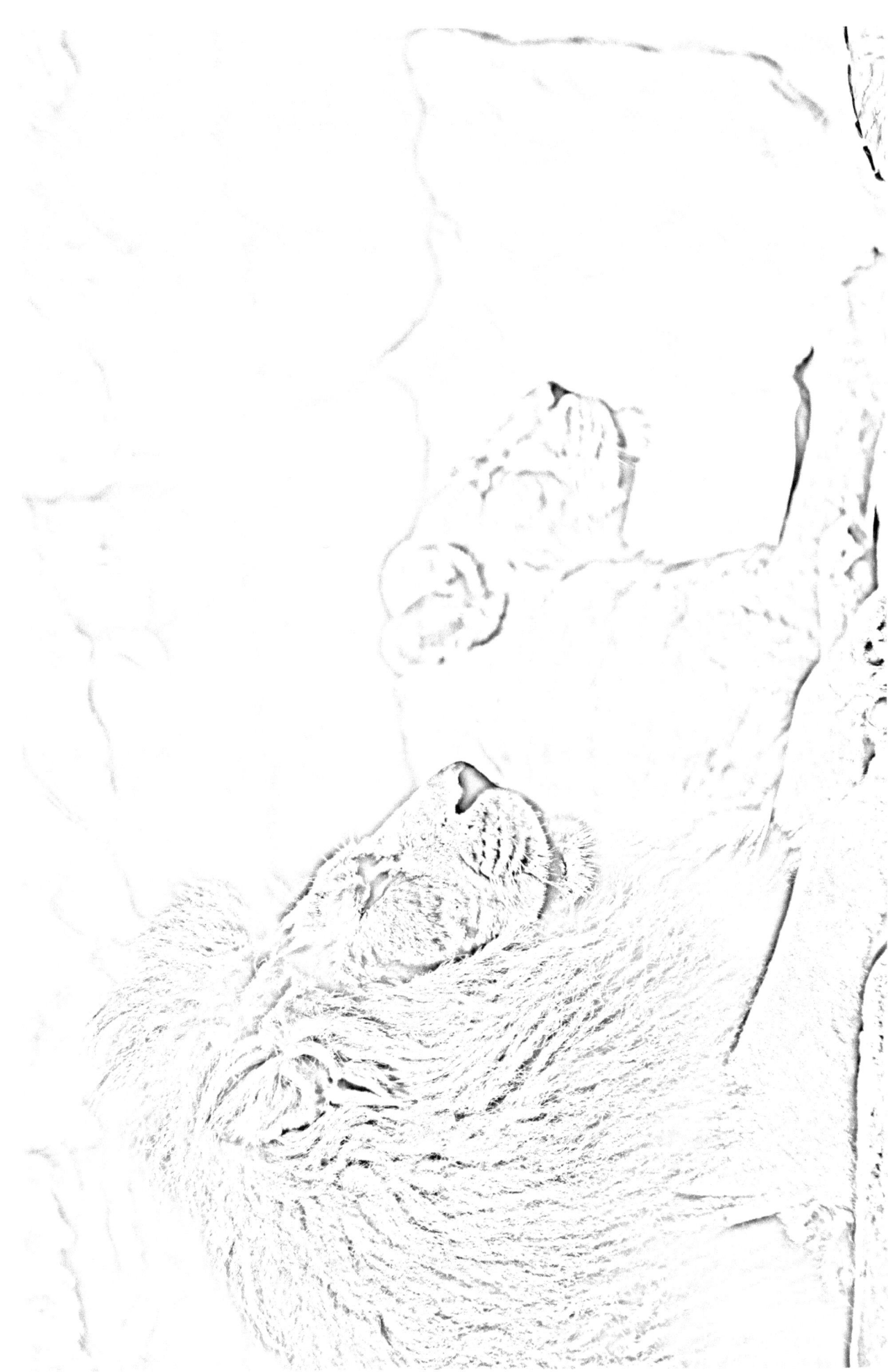

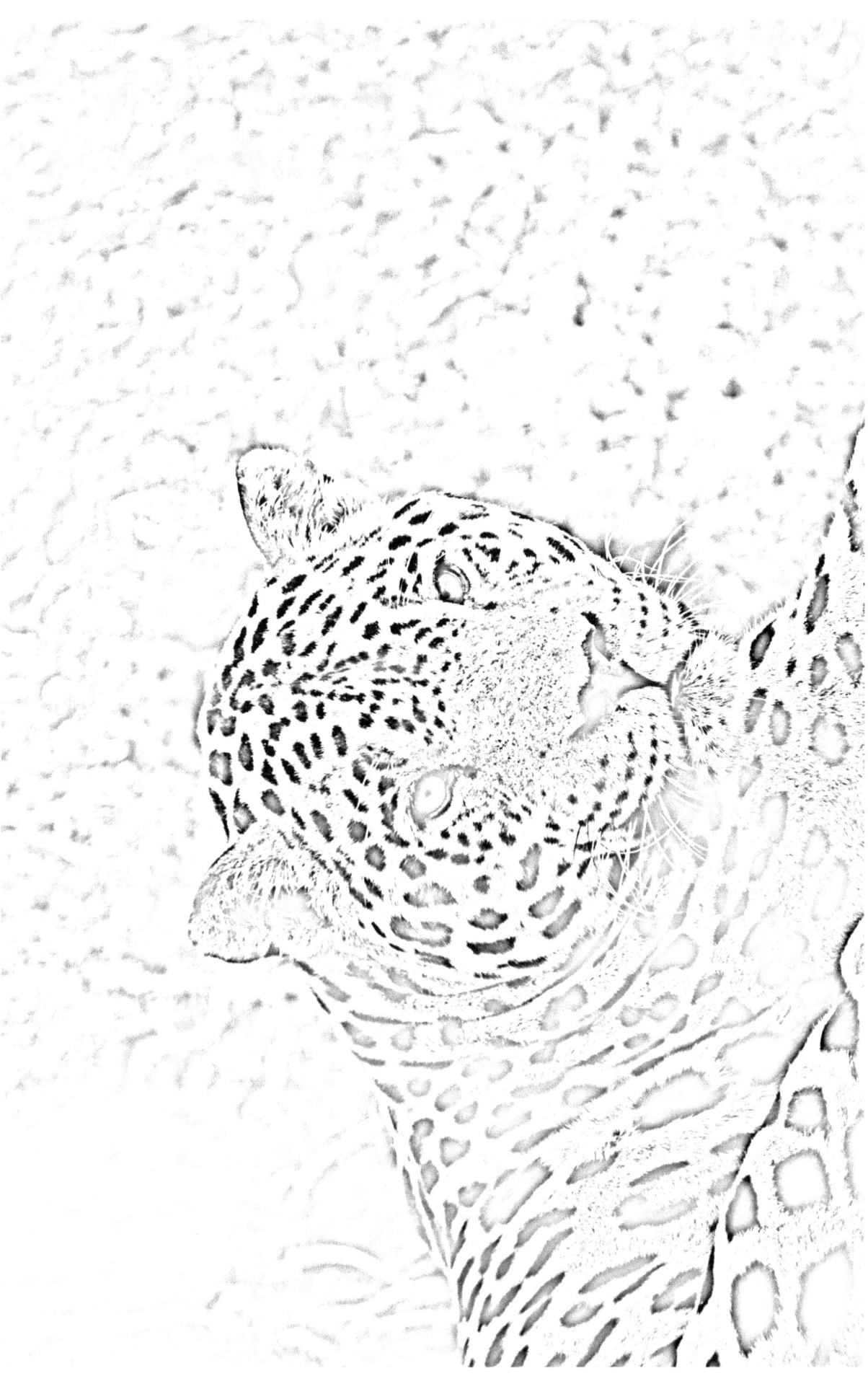

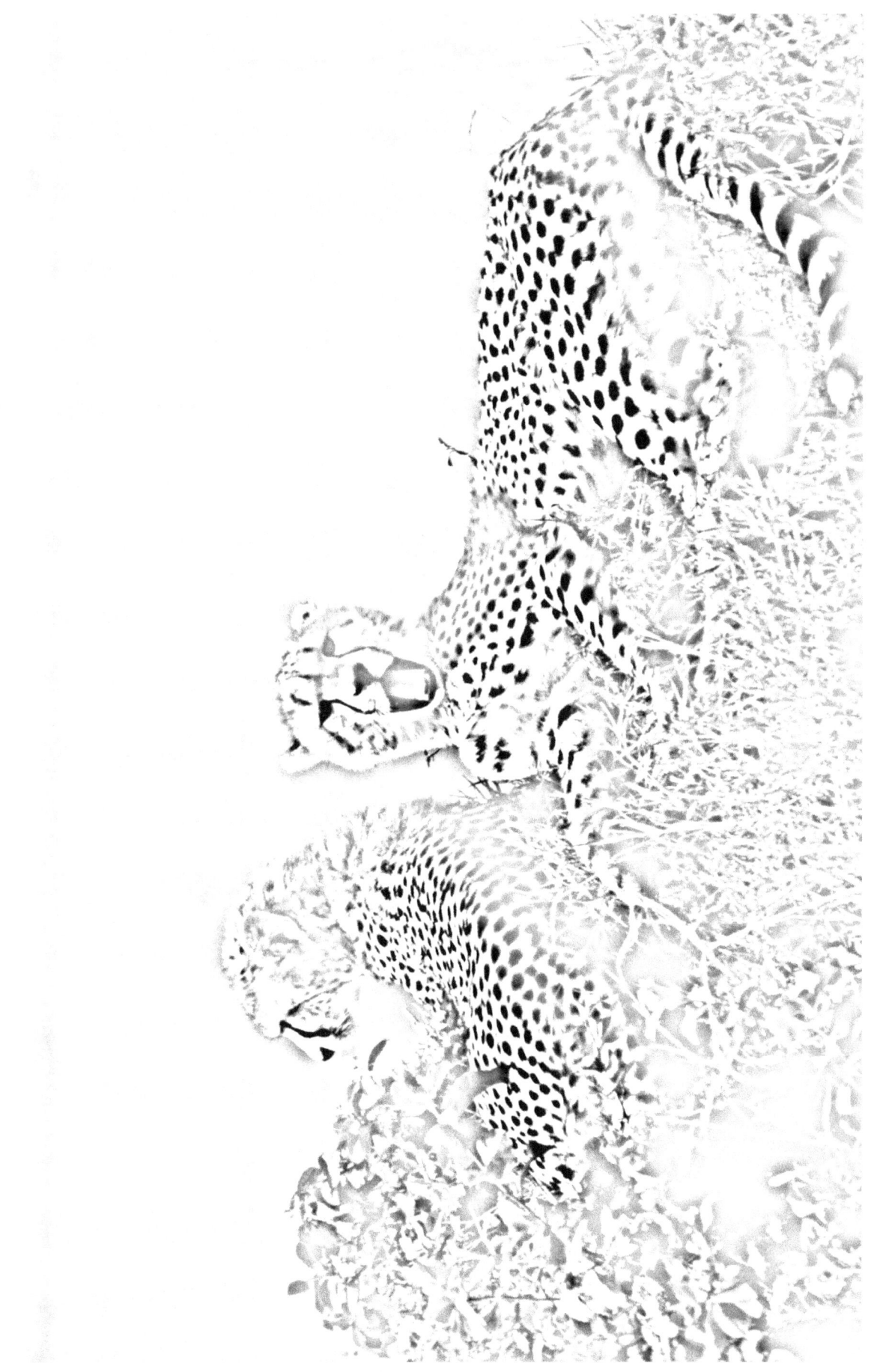

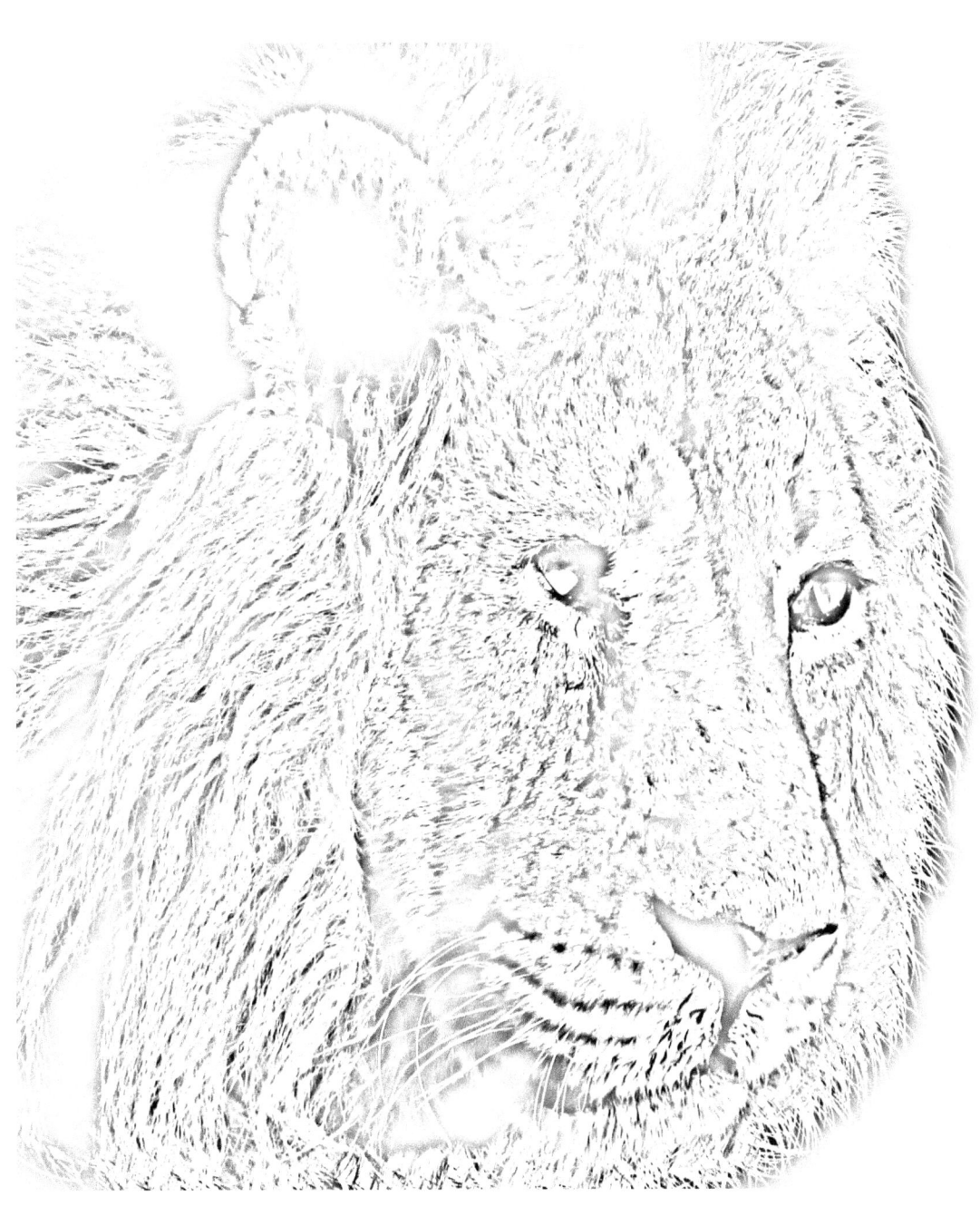

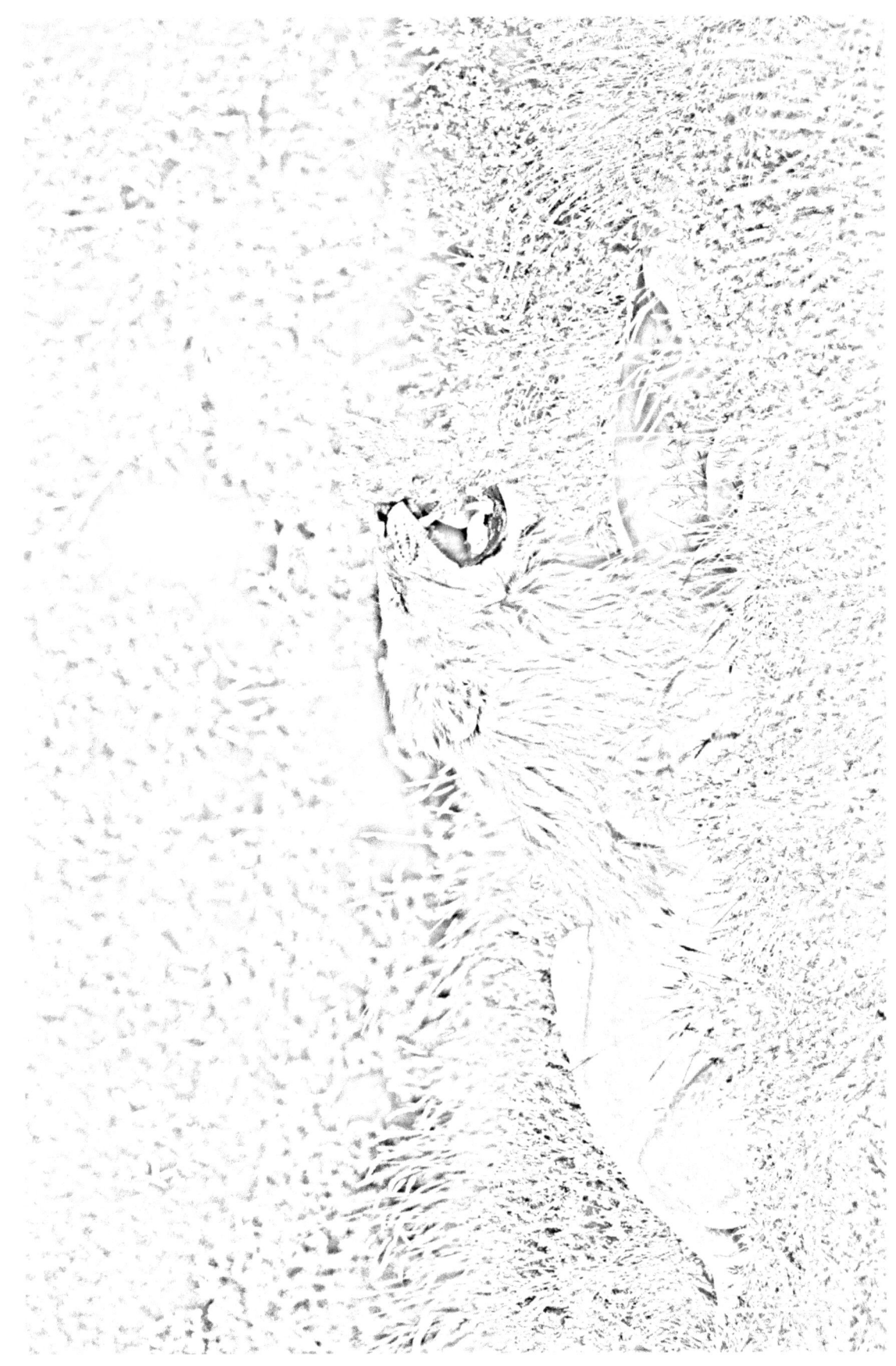

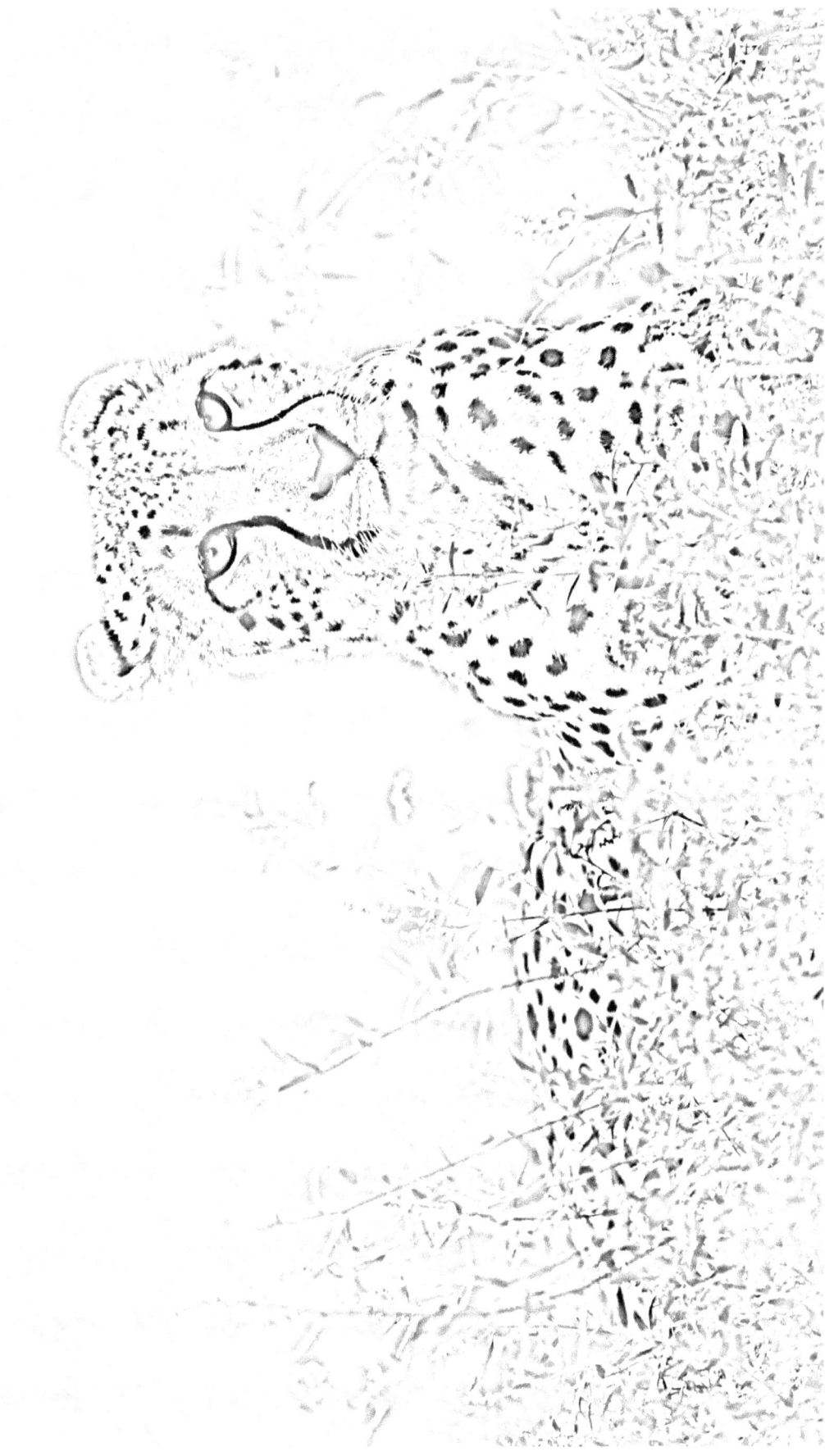

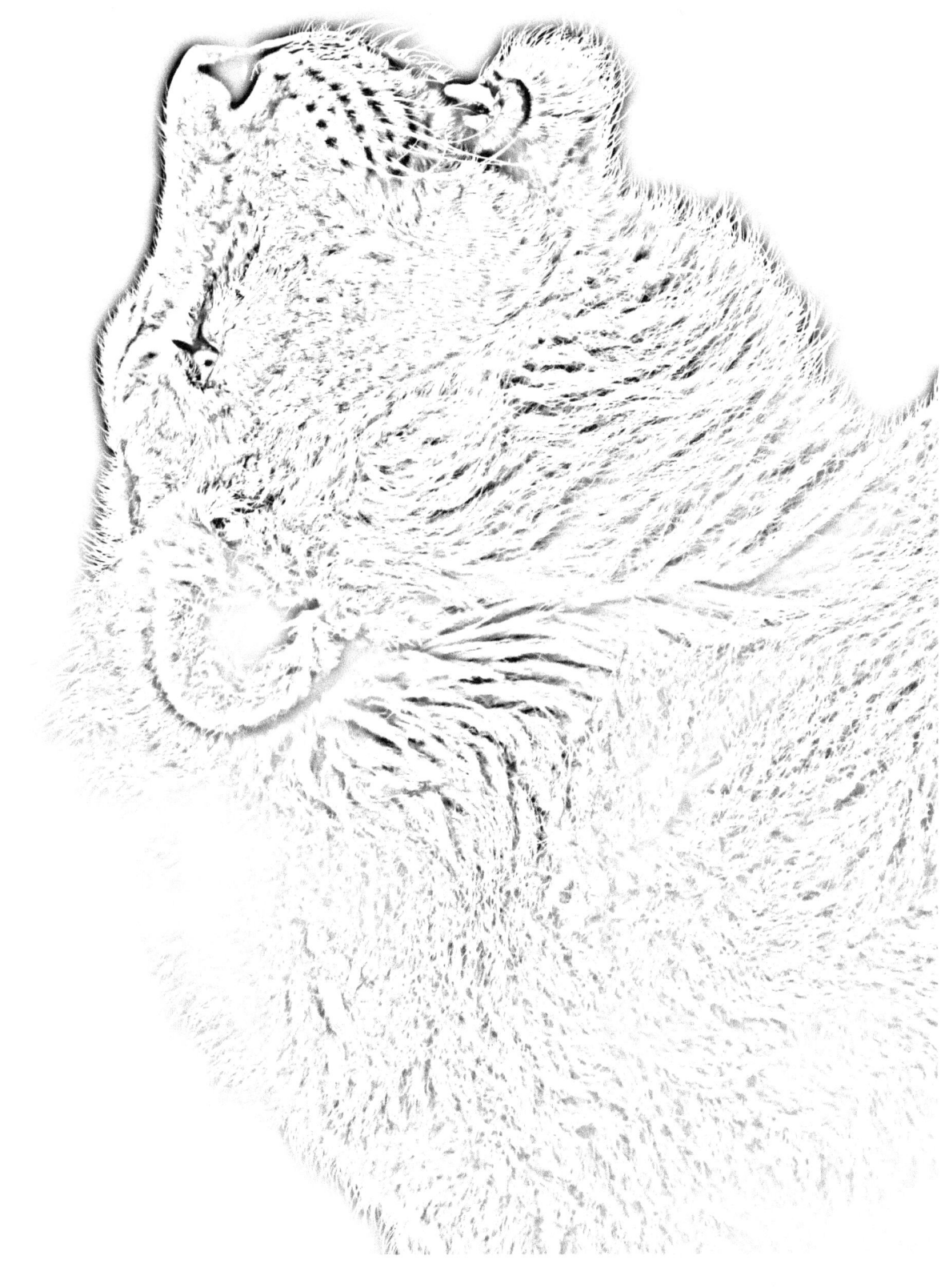

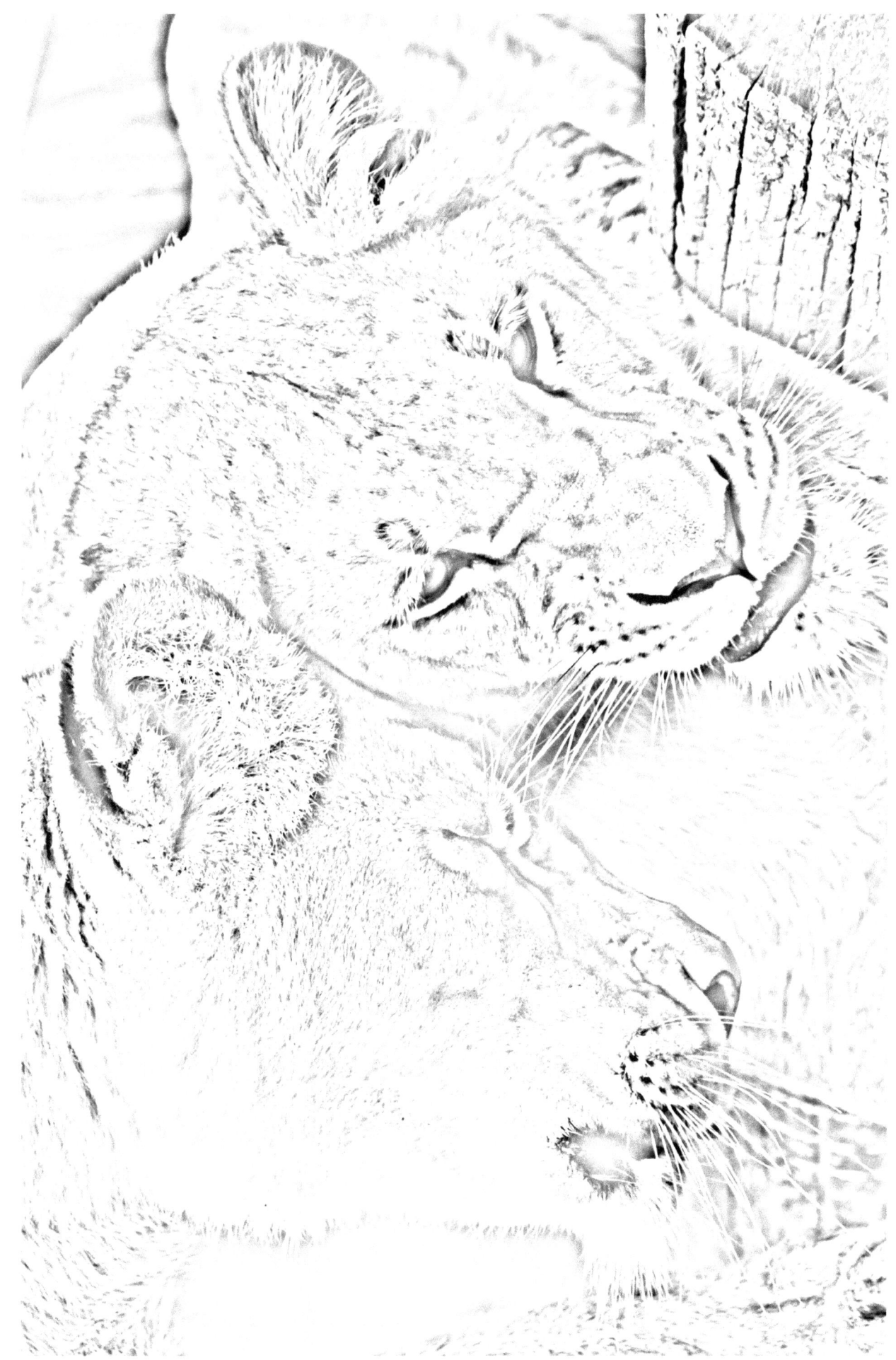

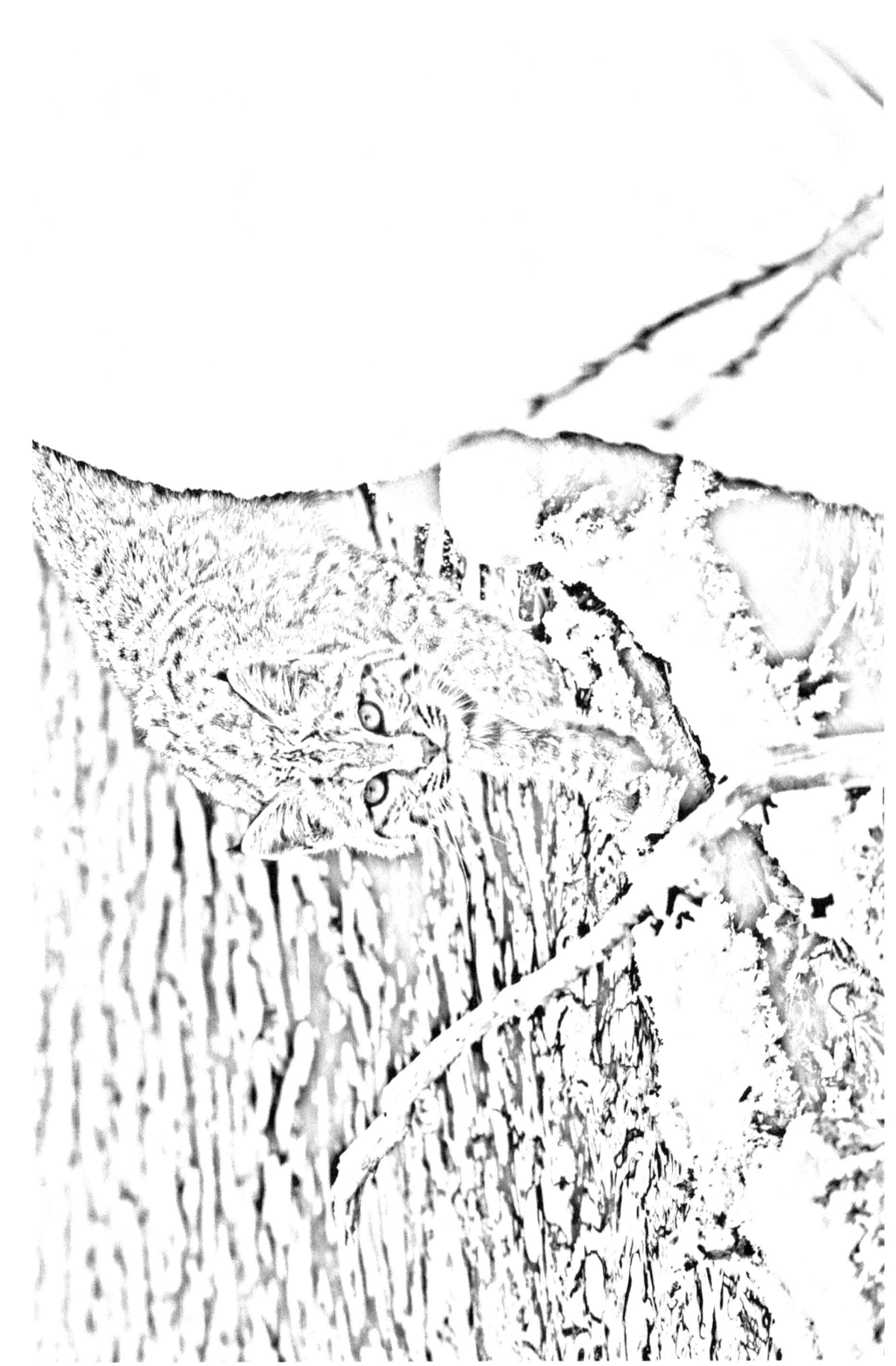

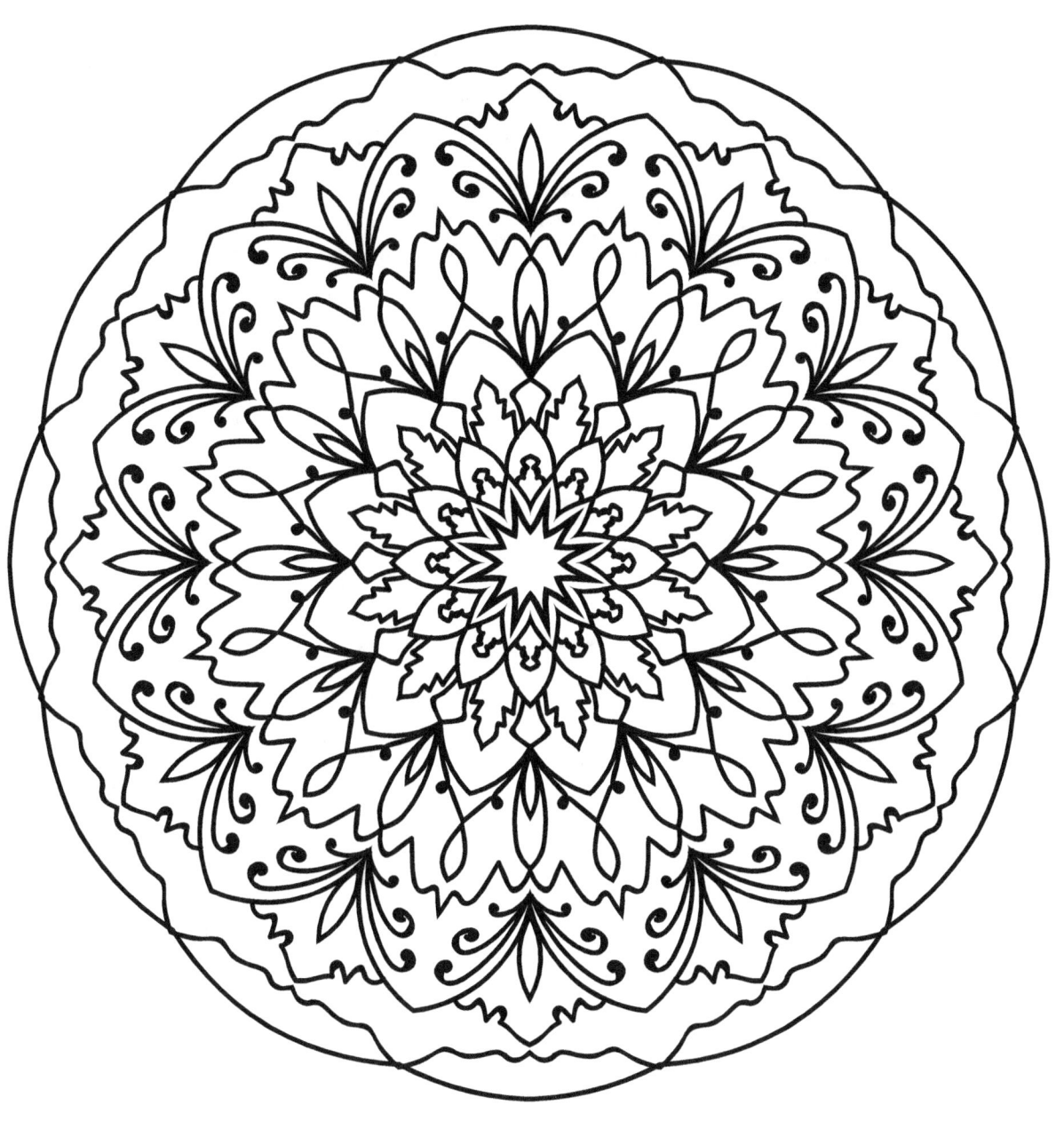

Look for other types of beautiful designs to color by author/illustrator Patricia Markham

(Mandala designs are featured in The Commuting Colorist Series - Books 1-5)

www.ingramcontent.com/pod-product-compliance
Lightning Source LLC
Chambersburg PA
CBHW062121220526
45471CB00010B/3822